Blockchain for Medical Research

Blockchain for Medical Research
Accelerating Trust in Healthcare

Sean T. Manion, PhD
Yaël Bizouati-Kennedy

CRC Press
Taylor & Francis Group
Boca Raton   London   New York

CRC Press is an imprint of the
Taylor & Francis Group, **an informa** business

A PRODUCTIVITY PRESS BOOK

First published 2020
by Routledge
52 Vanderbilt Avenue, New York, NY 10017

and by Routledge
2 Park Square, Milton Park, Abingdon, Oxon, OX14 4RN

Routledge is an imprint of the Taylor & Francis Group, an informa business

© 2020 Sean T. Manion, PhD and Yaël Bizouati-Kennedy

The right of Sean T. Manion, PhD and Yaël Bizouati-Kennedy to be identified as authors of this work has been asserted by them in accordance with sections 77 and 78 of the Copyright, Designs and Patents Act 1988.

Library of Congress Cataloging-in-Publication Data
Names: Manion, Sean T., author. | Bizouati-Kennedy, Yaël, author.
Title: Blockchain for medical research: accelerating trust in healthcare /
Sean T. Manion and Yaël Bizouati-Kennedy.
Description: Boca Raton: Taylor & Francis, 2020. |
Includes bibliographical references and index.
Identifiers: LCCN 2019053960 (print) | LCCN 2019053961 (ebook) |
ISBN 9780367347598 (hardback) | ISBN 9780367347468 (paperback) |
ISBN 9780429327735 (ebook)
Subjects: MESH: Computer Security | Healthcare Financing | Data Mining |
Electronic Health Records | Biomedical Research—economics |
Delivery of Health Care—economics
Classification: LCC RA440.85 (print) | LCC RA440.85 (ebook) | NLM W 26.5 |
DDC 362.10720285—dc23
LC record available at https://lccn.loc.gov/2019053960
LC ebook record available at https://lccn.loc.gov/2019053961

ISBN: 978-0-367-34746-8 (pbk)
ISBN: 978-0-367-34759-8 (hbk)
ISBN: 978-0-429-32773-5 (ebk)

Typeset in Garamond
by codeMantra

Contents

List of Figures

List of Tables

Preface

What is blockchain? While many have talked or written about it, and while I've been writing on the topic for a while, the answers tend to vary—depending on where you are on the evangelists-to-skeptics spectrum. When Sean offered me the chance to work with him on this book, one of my drivers was the fact that I believe in blockchain and what it will achieve. I don't believe this technology is a magic wand which will resolve all the world's problems and cure all ills.

Rather, I believe blockchain is an accelerator, of vision, ideas and truth.

While conducting research for this book, I had the privilege of interviewing several experts from different fields—technology, science, medicine, finance, philosophy—who each shed a different light on the question: what is blockchain?

In every fascinating conversation I had (I want to thank everyone who took the time to help in this research), everyone brought a different facet or aspect to the surface.

The common thread though is that blockchain provides one single source of truth. In a world increasingly full of noise, where thoughts are constantly shared, tweeted and broadcasted, where everything and everyone is measured by "followers" and "likes," it's hard to decipher not only what is true, but what matters. It's hard to cut through the noise.

Blockchain achieves that.

The second driver for me was a personal one, and the topic of the book: how then can blockchain help the healthcare field and medical science? How can blockchain help bring faster miracles?

I lost my almost 18-year-old son to schizophrenia. From the day my beautiful boy was diagnosed (January 3, 2012) to the day he died (February 29, 2012), few weeks elapsed. And for both him and me, this was a nanosecond. There were no miracles fast enough for him. In these few weeks, while

I tried to reassure myself, hoping a cure would be found shortly, hoping a miracle treatment would erase his mental pain and he would attend college, follow his dreams and become a musician or a neuroscientist, or both, I was also faced with reality: research was not being done fast enough, communication between various doctors was not being done fast enough. Nothing was fast enough but the progression of his mental illness.

For every parent faced with a child's critical illness, time is obviously of the essence. It's the difference between life and death. And this is what blockchain can achieve: hasten everything. Because this precept of having one single source of truth, when applied to healthcare, translates—for one—in faster research. Research that is verified, shared and distributed in a more efficient way. In turn, this means faster clinical trials and faster treatments for patients. This could also help contain the opioid pandemic. It will help bring back patients at the center of medicine. And this is only one example of the many ways this technology can ameliorate healthcare. And by "ameliorating," I mean, making it more accessible, faster and to more people.

Blockchain can and will bring faster miracles.

—YBK

My mother, Thomasina, died of cancer in May of 2017. It was a sad, sometimes horrible, sometimes beautiful, but ultimately tragic end of a great life. Excellent doctors and advances in medicine gave us a little more time, some wonderful moments, a little more music and some better quality of life at the end. But the miracles weren't fast enough for more. I am not alone in this experience and cancer is not the only culprit. Our time is limited. A little more life, a little more experience, a little more achievement and a little better quality of life is the ultimate value. Money is great, but it is not enough. Steve Jobs died rich at 56, leaving humanity a little poorer, and his loved ones much poorer in their grief. In business, time may be money, but in life, money doesn't buy time.

What if we could speed up science, improve the quality of research for fewer wrong turns and wasted effort and reduce the overall cost of execution improving the return on investment of research? What if we could give more time, better quality of life and more chance of long-term reprieve to those families dealing with cancer? What if we could improve the quality of life and outcomes for the veteran with a traumatic brain injury and his spouse and three kids? What if we could extend the time a university professor with Alzheimer's could continue to teach our kids and enjoy time with her family? What if we could cure childhood disease allowing kids to grow up, achieve their dreams and change the world?

That is the overarching goal of this book, to bring the worlds of science and blockchain together, advance medical research and improve health outcomes. It is not a deep dive into one subject, but rather a view across topics in simple language to allow experts in technology, science and medicine (along with everybody else) to understand the possibilities as exploration of this intersection gets underway in the real world. We offer cross visibility of where we are: the nascent power of this rapidly emerging technology and the complex challenges of medical research, and we unite them in a vision for the future where science is not only trusted, but also better because it is verifiable by blockchain.

—**STM**

Acknowledgments

I want to acknowledge some of the people who brought me into the blockchain space and guided me along the way. John Reusing of Bad Decisions/ Baltimore Bitcoin fame first introduced me to the concept. Debbie Bucci and the dozens of contributors to the 2016 HHS ONC blockchain and healthcare white paper contest showed me the possibilities. Lauren Long led the first foray into blockchain for neuroscience research at Society for Neuroscience 2017. Reem El Seed introduced me to human centered design. Felicia Qashu helped me dissect research into its component parts, while building an analog trust network of research at Defense and Veterans Brain Injury Center. Loretta Polite helped me get my head around the regulatory challenges and possibilities. Heather Flannery helped me explore the blockchain for research vision and continues to pursue this shared vision on a parallel path. Samson Williams provided the much needed common sense and business perspective while reminding us that "blockchain isn't hot sauce, you can't just put that sh*t on everything." Nicole Tay was my New York City blockchain guide while providing technical and ethical perspective along the way. Natalie Marler gave me deeper publishing insights. Susan Ramonat, John Bass and Jose Arrieta shared their brilliant insights and inspired with their industry leadership. Thanks to Gilles Hilary and Georgetown University for hosting our Blockchain in Health Research conferences. Thanks also to Jacob Kean and University of Utah for facilitating the early real-world explorations of this tech for research.

These are just a handful of the hundreds of technologists, entrepreneurs, researchers, patients, providers, regulators, conference planners, attendees and everybody else that have informed my thinking and expanded the field and the possibilities for better science and faster miracles that helped make this book possible.

I would also like to profoundly thank Yaël for coming along with me on this journey. Her perspective and voice as a journalist allowed us to complete a wide-ranging tour of multiple technical areas (without an endless dive down every possible rabbit hole) in an accessible way for a broad audience, while also allowing for numerous interviews with experts across the key areas.

Finally I want to thank my wife Katie for her endless patience and thoughtful insight, along with my family and friends for their support as I've delved into this new blockchain world (and for thier tolerance as I've pulled them along from time to time).

—STM

This book has been one of the most challenging, intellectually stimulating and exhilarating projects I've ever worked on.

First, I want to thank Sean for his leap of faith. It takes a special kind of person to entrust a journalist with limited scientific background to work on a book specifically addressing ways to re-instill trust in the scientific process. While the irony is worth noting, I like to remember that at the core of every technological advance—there is (still) humanity.

I am also deeply grateful for all the people I interviewed for this book. All these experts from various fields, not only took the time to share their insights, but also their passion and vision for a better world. On a personal note, I am deeply appreciative for the way each of these conversations took fascinating, unexpected twists and turns, broaden my world and views and expanded my mind.

Thank you, Jose Arrieta, Phil Baker, John Bass, Brian Behlendorf, Alex Cahana, Wendy Charles, Karmen Condic-Jurkic, Helen Disney, Heather Leigh Flannery, Tiffany Gray, David Houlding, David Metcalf, Susan Ramonat, Yauheni Solad and Nicole Tay.

Finally, I want to thank my amazing husband, Paul, for his love, support and immense patience.

And of course, I want to thank my beautiful son Keanu, who watches over me from high above, who continues to inspire me and will always be the wind beneath my wings.

—YBK

Authors

Sean T. Manion, PhD is a neuroscientist who spent nearly two decades in military health research and administration. He is now the Chief Scientific Officer at ConsenSys Health, co-editor of the journal *Blockchain for Science* published by Frontiers and co-founder of the non-profits Science Distributed and Blockchain in Healthcare Global, part of the IEEE International Standards & Technology Organization. Sean is a member of the HIMSS Blockchain Task Force, a member of the IEEE Standards Association "Standards for the Framework of Distributed Ledger Technology (DLT) Use in Healthcare and the Life and Social Sciences (P2418.6)," a fellow of the British Blockchain Association and serves on the editorial review board for the peer-reviewed journals *Ledger*, the *Journal of the British Blockchain Association* and *Frontiers in Blockchain*.

He lives in The Bronx, NY with distributed time in Pittsburgh, Baltimore and DC.

Yaël Bizouati-Kennedy is a former full-time financial journalist and editor. Her work has appeared in *The Wall Street Journal*, *Financial News*, *The Financial Times*, *Business Insider* and several other publications. She also worked as vice president-senior content writer for New York-based financial services firms, including New York Life and MSCI, where she led thought leadership efforts around several platforms. Most recently, she has been freelancing and writes among other things, about blockchain. Yaël holds a master's degree in journalism from New York University and a master's degree in Russian Studies/Russian Politics from Université Toulouse Jean Jaurès.

She originally hails from Toulouse, France.

Introduction

At its core, science is the foundation of shared human knowledge about the natural world. Scientific research is the systematic study of the world around and inside us, allowing for new innovations to be applied to nearly every industry and human endeavor. Globally, we spend more than $1.7 trillion annually on research and development across all industries. More than $300 billion of this sum is spent on medical research alone, half in the United States, with the goal of contributing more evidence to evidence-based medicine and finding discoveries that can improve health and save lives.

The advancement of medical knowledge and treatment relies on the science that underlies it being correct and reproducible. As argued in, "Science will be Blockchained by 2025":

> At the foundation of the scientific process is the expectation of reproducible results. This comes from trust in the integrity and verifiability of the data. Unfortunately, the pace of scientific advancement and the current incentive systems have led to numerous problems: falsified data, lack of reproducibility and limitations of peer-review to name a few. These problems have become increasingly prominent and threaten to undermine the infrastructure we use to advance knowledge. The problems with science also threaten to undermine the trust in institutions we rely on to manage the hundreds of billions of dollars we invest every year in research. [1]

A huge problem in health-related research is that significant portions of the findings intended to contribute to the advancement of medical treatments are not reproducible. This is wasted time, money and effort. What's worse is that it is difficult if not impossible in the current system to identify this portion of bad science. It goes undetected as noise in the system or bad data that continues to infect future funding decisions and research. The impact of this is a declining return on investment for medical research and declining trust in the research itself. As we spend more to live longer and better, we get less from our efforts because of the systemic inefficiencies.

A key framework for the solution to this problem has been around for decades and mirrors the foundation of modern science itself. The Open Science movement is a structured return to the original transparency that made scientific research the most powerful tool in the toolbox of human effort for centuries. The challenge is that as an idea it works, but in practice, it has not been widely successful in altering the misaligned incentive systems (e.g., graduate degrees, tenure, publishing and funding) that have become commonplace in science as it has scaled tremendously in the last 75 years since World War II. Open Science has not yet demonstrated the value proposition necessary for enough traction to change research on an enterprise level, and this is true especially in health and medicine.

What's new however, is that now, we have an array of emerging technologies that are advancing and maturing at the right time to play critical roles in improving science and accelerating research. Emerging technologies, especially blockchain and other distributed ledger technologies, are a suite of new tools that have been rapidly demonstrating value in several industries across many different types of use case. Blockchain can be applied at multiple levels to assist science and the Open Science movement toward a more effective process of advancing new discoveries, knowledge and application to solving real-world problems.

The purpose of this book is to give scientists, healthcare providers, technologists, health and research administrators, and the general public an overview of

1. Blockchain and its value to different sectors including health and research.
2. Science, its value to advancing medicine and health outcomes, and the growing problems with medical research that are impeding this progress.
3. Insight into how blockchain can be applied to medical research to improve our evidence-based medicine as well as our health and well-being.

In Part I, "Blockchain Isn't Tech," we explore the fundamentals of blockchain and make the argument that while it has a critical technology component the bulk of the application is dependent on the network of human users and the governance they have agreed upon for the processes where the tech is applied. Chapter 1, "Distributed Ledgers," looks at the idea of a distributed ledger and the history of precursors to the current emergence of blockchain and other distributed ledger technologies. Chapter 2, "Blockchain Basics," looks at the basics of blockchain and cryptocurrency applications from a non-technical perspective. Chapter 3, "From Finance to Health: Way Beyond Bitcoin," explores the expanding application of blockchain beyond cryptocurrency in the financial, supply chain, manufacturing and healthcare industries. Chapter 4, "Data Complexities," highlights the challenges in translating the basic cryptocurrency model of blockchain to areas of increasingly complex data, with a focus on health and research data. Chapter 5, "Blockchain Is People," looks at the need for a network of users to bring the most value from a blockchain solution and why this is truer in health science than in other areas.

In Part II, "Science Is Easy," we will explore science's value and challenges. Chapter 6, "Good Science," looks briefly at the history of science and the scientific method, what science looks like as a process, and the benefits science has brought to society. Chapter 7, "Evidence-Based Medicine," looks at how health science delivers advances in evidence-based medicine. Chapter 8, "Science Crisis," explores the problems with health science, specifically focusing on the delays that are involved in the 17 years it takes to go from "bench to bedside" and the 20% or more of the $150 million/year in U.S. health science research that is not reproducible. Chapter 9, "Open Science," sets the foundation that the Open Science movement has identified key areas and approaches to improve and accelerate science, but that progress has been limited because it lacks the key tools to overcome the current incentive system in science.

In Part III "DAO of Science," we will cover the concept of a distributed autonomous organization (DAO) and make the argument that this type of structure will be most suitable for core medical research to function optimally. We will lay out a vision of what this could look like in the future along with a roadmap of how to get there from where we currently are.

Chapter 10, "Distributing Science," outlines blockchain applications to science across the eight areas using a mission essential task list (METL) to break science down into its core eight tasks and subsequent sub-tasks to better understand the process. Chapter 11, "Better Quality Science," focuses on how and where a distributed approach can improve the quality of science and the costs and benefits of this approach. Chapter 12, "Value-Based Research," explores the idea of return on investment of health research and the increases that can be gained through a distributed approach. Chapter 13, "Faster Medical Miracles," reveals the advances of a distributed approach to health science to accelerating the steps that currently take 17 years to go from idea to cure. Chapter 14, "DAO of Science," reveals a vision of the future of a DAO for health science and outlines a roadmap of how to get there.

Chapter 15, "The Roadmap," looks at the future of science and what this can look like, along with a rough strategic plan of how to get there.

Throughout the book we have woven in the critical insights of more than a dozens of experts from science, health and technology based on recent interviews conducted on the topics we have covered. This is intended to give the reader a more connected context to these areas as well as enhance the overall vision of the future.

The goal of all of this is to give any reader, regardless of background, a fundamental understanding of our current system of science and medicine, the basics of the new tools and opportunities that blockchain give these efforts, and the vision and roadmap for an achievable future state that gives us better science, better research value and faster medical miracles to save lives.

Thank you for your time and attention.

BLOCKCHAIN ISN'T TECH

I

Blockchain has a key technology component, but in any complex data application such as health and science, it is more about the network of users and shared data governance.

Chapter 1

Distributed Ledgers

From analog ledgers to digital applications of the idea, in the form of blockchain and other distributed ledger technology (DLT), the goal of multiple parties having separate records, rather than a single party being the holder of truth, has been a way of ensuring trust for many centuries. How this use has evolved and is now beginning to rapidly take hold across industries is critical as a foundation for where it has been and can be used in scientific research and advancing medical knowledge.

Distributed Ledgers

Distributed ledgers are nothing new. They actually have been around for centuries. Blockchain has simply created a framework for having a secured, shared system of distributed ledgers, which is digitized to enable rapid, automated synchronization across the entire distributed system. Before we start looking at the modern emergence of blockchain and other distributed ledger technologies, let's look at what they are, the forms they can take, as well as their value.

In its most basic form, a distributed ledger is any record of events shared among a group or a network with some measure of synchronization of the contents. This record of events allows the group to have a common point of reference of what has occurred with the contents of the ledger. This generally allows for some level of agreement on the accuracy and authority of that ledger to be the foundation of future action (i.e., assigning or resolving possession/ownership in the case of ledger tracking resources).

In the case of two parties, this may be relatively straightforward, but if there is a lack of trust, it may require a third party to be the arbiter of what is transcribed in the ledger. This objective shared or agreed-upon authority becomes more critical if a greater number of parties are involved. The trusted third party—or objective additional party—becomes the final authority on what the ledger records and in resolving disputes. For example, banks, accountants, government entities and courts have become the trusted third party for many shared ledgers.

Traditionally, the trusted third party has been the central node in a centralized network framework. This allows for uniformity of connection and verification, but at the cost of a single point of delay or failure in the centralized node. A decentralized node framework avoids the single point of delay or failure, but at the cost of uneven distribution and even limited access by isolated parts of a network. A distributed network allows peer-to-peer connection across all parties, allowing the most versatile and robust connection of the three, and with no inherent trust mechanism such as a trusted third party (Figure 1.1).

The core value of a distributed ledger is that it allows for an agreed-upon record of past events as a shared basis for future action. This is the foundation of cooperation and agreement for most action in human history. A shared ledger—the master version of which is kept and authorized by a centralized third party before being distributed—has been the standard for most of civilization. The problem with this system is the potential corruptibility of that centralized source of the ledger, either through poor maintenance or through open malfeasance. While the original goal of this type of centralized system is to create some ability for moving forward based on a shared record of events, some of the downsides are that first it enables a tremendous amount of bad behavior or perceived bad behavior by those in the central authority: downsides that manifest themselves in banking and government corruption for example. A second downside is the slow

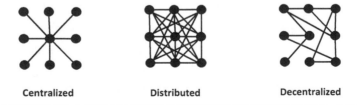

Centralized   Distributed   Decentralized

Figure 1.1   Network frameworks: a comparison of the node distribution across three generalized models of network connection.

speed and high (and exploitable) cost of maintaining that central authority. This can delay action and limit resources even when there is minimal bad behavior, whether real or perceived.

A distributed ledger that does not rely on a centralized authority to stay synchronized in its contents allows for higher trust among the parties using the ledger. The degree of trust will depend on the level of shared governance and immutability of the contents. With the emergence of blockchain and other distributed ledger technologies, we now have the ability to introduce this type of third party-less shared system creating higher levels of trust among parties involved and new degrees of speed, low cost and high-fidelity data. At its core, blockchain provides a framework to re-establish trust.

Brian Behlendorf, executive director of Hyperledger, an open-source collaborative effort created to advance cross-industry blockchain technologies started by The Linux Foundation, tells us, for example, that the reason you don't want a centralized solution is how do you really know who runs the central server?

In a conversation, Brian said that the main factor for deciding whether to use blockchain is, "is there a trustworthy entity for this use case?" According to him, the key driver for blockchain is more political than technical.

"So, you really need a blockchain when you have a scenario where the participants in a space want to avoid an all-empowering actor, where there's one key position and everybody is slave to it," he notes. "The need for this will grow as we move toward a world we want more entrusting."

Emergence of Blockchain

In 2009, in the wake of the global banking collapse, a new model for an electronic cash system was introduced by an anonymous person or persons under the name Satoshi Nakamoto in a white paper [1-1], outlining the system. It was based on a distributed ledger system that encrypted transactions into blocks of information of what exchanges or transactions had taken place. These encrypted transactions were then verified by the entire network of users to authenticate them in a process called mining. The reward for mining—spending the time and energy contributing to authenticating the record—was to award electronic cash—the cryptocurrency known as bitcoin—to the miners. A random miner would receive a bitcoin for each block of transactions that was verified and completed. Completed blocks were then mathematically hashed as the foundation of the next block to chain each new block to the existing record. None of these records could be tampered without altering the hash of the block containing it in subsequent blocks, thereby creating a red flag that would cause the miners to invalidate the record. This system of chaining blocks of records allowed for a trusted record with no intermediary third party.

Many of the pieces and ideas of the Bitcoin paper, including the blockchain foundation, had been developed earlier. What Satoshi accomplished is that s/he pulled them together in a unique and functional way, with new insights on solving what was called the double-spend problem (a party in the system sending/spending a single coin to two separate parties simultaneously to cheat the system). This combination created the first viable electronic cash system, Bitcoin, based on a technology that would commonly become referred to as blockchain.

Bitcoin was the first functional electronic cash system and the first widely utilized application of blockchain technology. It wasn't the first time either of these concepts was explored. The idea of an encrypted, fully electronic cash system (not simply an electronic transfer of dollars or other existing currency) had been around almost as long as the internet allowed for listservs and discussion boards. The idea gained more structure and popularity in the mid-1990s with the publication of works such as Timothy May's "Cyphernomicon" (1994) [1-2] and James Bell's "Assassination Politics" (1996) [1-3]. The idea of encrypted electronic cash advanced in more mainstream literature in Neal Stephenson's "Cryptonomicon" (1999) [1-4]. These explorations continued to feed growing discussion on the topic by technology and cryptography enthusiasts for years.

Meanwhile, in the early 1990s, cryptographers Stuart Haber and Scott Stornetta developed what would become known as the first blockchain [1-5]. They published their initial ideas on its use for time-stamping documents for intellectual property purposes in 1991 in the *Journal of Cryptography* [1-6], along with additional papers on the topic over the next several years. They even began printing the hash of the first blockchain in the *New York Times* each week, a distributed though not (at that time yet) digital ledger.

The popularization of blockchain applications for an electronic cash system and elsewhere in the financial industry has been the foundation for a tremendous amount of research and development (R&D) on blockchain and other distributed ledger technologies. The monetization and explosion of value of bitcoin and other cryptocurrencies, including ether, litecoin and ripple to name a few of an ever-expanding list, has underwritten the cost of much of the early R&D and expanded the field of skilled developers exploring other uses. Without these cryptocurrency and financial technology applications, there would not be the worldwide public and private exploration of blockchain across many use cases and industries.

But while this financial foundation has allowed the field to grow, it is important to remember that it is not the only or even the original area of application. Nicole Tay, a blockchain consultant, made a point to tell us that the changes in blockchain will happen thanks to and through the financial world.

"Fintech moves so much faster than [scientific] research does, so changes will come from there. And as they integrate their systems it will become impossible for us in research to not do it also," Nicole tells us.

What is crucial to underline is that what we have in blockchain is a new tool, or suite of tools, that can be applied in different ways to different problems. By exploring these technologies more broadly, taking them apart, finding trade-offs for each use and finding lessons learned across industries, it will enable more value to be derived in their application and more problems to be solved with their implementation. While blockchain is not a cure-all, it is a multi-varied tool for an array of different problem areas.

Other Distributed Ledger Technologies

While originally used in the early 1990s in reference to the work of Haber and Stornetta, blockchain as a term has become most closely aligned with its use in relation to Bitcoin. Some prefer to use the term only for those applications they feel have reached a sufficient point of decentralization, while more commonly it has become used colloquially for an array of distributed ledger technologies. There are advantages one gets from less decentralization including growth, scalability, limited or permissioned access, speed, lower cost and flexibility. At the same time, these centralized, partial applications of the technology do not realize the full potential of a fully distributed ledger with no centralized point of potential manipulation or failure.

For many industries and use cases, it may be necessary to utilize centralization as training wheels or scaffolding, while a more fully distributed solution is developed where possible.

Chapter 2

Blockchain Basics

Blockchain requires technical depth to create, yet only some basic fundamentals to understand how and where it can transform different industries. As with any new technology that scales beyond first adopter use, there are key principles that need to be grasped generally in order to fit into the context of current operations for a business or industry. It is then critical to have cross-discipline team's understanding of both the technical digital aspects and the details of the data and workflow of the subject matter at hand.

What Is Blockchain?

The technical details of blockchain are critical to any successful implementation but are beyond the scope of this book; much like the fundamentals of car engine design and repair are critical to a successful road trip, but not necessarily the focus of every driver or passenger. Here is the briefest of overviews on the details to give the reader some frame of reference. We would encourage you to explore numerous books and courses on the technical details for a deeper understanding of those aspects (Figure 2.1).

At the core of a basic blockchain, such as the Bitcoin blockchain, is a ledger of records of transactions or data exchanges between uniquely identified network of nodes or users. Each transaction or exchange of data is recorded, and a specified volume of transaction makes up a block. This block is then given a unique identifier or hash via a mathematical function or hash function. This hash is a 256-character encryption in the standard SHA256 encryption of the Bitcoin blockchain. Other encryption standards are available in

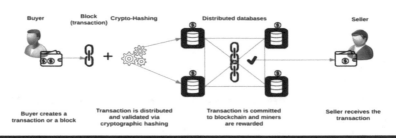

Figure 2.1   Basic blockchain diagram: a simplified look at the key elements of a blockchain network (Creative Commons license: B140970324 [CC BY-SA 4.0 (https://creativecommons.org/licenses/by-sa/4.0)] https://commons.wikimedia.org/wiki/File:Blockchain-Process.png.)

other systems. The hash is unique to the transaction data that make up the block. Any alteration, no matter how minor, in the transaction data will result in a completely different hash for that block. Each block of transactions is hashed, and this hash is the first piece of data for the next block. Any alteration to older blocks will impact the hash in the next block, changing that block's data and therefore its hash as well. This means even the smallest alterations in any block will alter every subsequent block, like dominoes. This makes the chain of blocks, or blockchain, highly tamper-proof.

Every block in the system is validated by the network before it is incorporated into the blockchain. This is called proofing. There are various ways this proofing can occur. The Bitcoin blockchain uses a process called proof-of-work. This has the network nodes act as validators of the new block by running a program to solve a mathematical equation. In this case, it is essentially predicting the hash for that block. This is referred to as mining and the network nodes as miners. The miner who finds the mathematical solution, which is complex enough to occur almost at random across the network each time, is rewarded with an electronic coin also known as a bitcoin.

This proof-of-work model has proven very resilient and secure over the past decade. Given the size of the Bitcoin network, it has made the ledger of transactions in the Bitcoin blockchain virtually tamper-proof. The trade-off is that the large network of miners is very energy dependent. This has led to the development of a variety of other systems, blockchain and other distributed ledger approaches, with differing types of proofs and levels off security. This world of trade-offs is still advancing but is a critical area to understand when diving deeper and identifying specific approaches to solving specific problems.

It is often summarized in three key variable areas: transparency, security and scalability. Transparency is high in the Bitcoin blockchain, as everyone who joins has access to the entire log of recorded transactions. This type of public blockchain is desirable for many functions where eliminating the cost and control of a third-party intermediary is the goal.

Other blockchains and distributed ledger solutions are less transparent, with permissioned public blockchains having some barrier to entry beyond just the basic technical competency, and private blockchains (that may not even meet some technical definitions of blockchain, but are some form of distributed ledger solution) having some level of control by centralized parties.

With respect to security, there are various threats to consider when looking at blockchains along with associated trade-offs. A blockchain is resilient from physical threat by distributing the entire ledger across all nodes in the system. Unlike a centralized or even a backed-up centralized database, there is a negligible threat of physical destruction of the data with so many copies. From a tampering security standpoint, a public blockchain like Bitcoin with many nodes involved in verification is highly robust against tampering. A smaller network can be compromised if enough of the nodes are controlled by one party allowing them to control 51% of the network. This majority ownership could potentially allow them to falsely verify a tampered record. In the case of Bitcoin, this would require hacking millions of computers around the world simultaneously. For a smaller blockchain network, it may only require a handful. In the case of a private blockchain, it would be vulnerable to tampering by those who maintain the access and control of the system. In general, this is why these private systems are more geared toward internal or consortia-based groups where some level of trust is already established (and also why some don't like to refer to them as real blockchains, even when they maintain that type of ledger system).

It is worth noting that there are sometimes reports and concerns of blockchains being hacked. In reality, the type of 51% attacks described above is rare and generally only occurs in smaller, more vulnerable systems that have not set up appropriate cybersecurity architecture for their overall enterprise, including balancing network access with value in the system. Just like you wouldn't store piles of cash in a bank vault that wasn't yet finished with construction, you need to be cautious about anticipating security issues before placing anything of value within a system. If the cost of hacking the system is significantly lower than the value of hacking it, someone will likely try. In most cases of blockchain hacking, loss or theft, the fault actually lies not with the blockchain but with an individual user (i.e., losing password/key) or third-party exchange company hired to handle the technical details of the blockchain interface for convenience purposes.

When it comes to scalability, there are two factors to consider: the speed of transactions that a particular blockchain system can handle and the overall cost to operate that system. In the case of Bitcoin and many open blockchains, the speed of transaction is somewhat limited. A private blockchain, or a distributed system that trades full ledger distribution for speed, can execute transactions much more quickly but won't have the same attributes of transparency and security. When it comes to cost of operation, the bigger and more comprehensive the network, the more resources it costs to maintain. For a private blockchain system, that means both user network and any centralized components. For a public system, the cost can be more evenly distributed across a network (everyone who joins has their own computer or at least a central processing unit (CPU)/graphics processing unit (GPU)), but there may still be an energy usage cost to the whole system that could be considerable. By some estimates, the Bitcoin network, with its full transparency and huge network proof-of-work system as security, uses as much energy as a small industrialized country.

One of the most significant pieces of value of a blockchain is the peer-to-peer sharing of information in the ledger. This provides the redundancy (multiple identical copies) and resiliency to maintain the ledger in multiple locations, and also provides an amazing aspect of speed and efficiency in data sharing. An excellent example of this is the U.S. Department of Health and Human Services' Accelerate blockchain-based acquisition program, which was piloted in 2018 and received the first ever authority to operate (ATO, meaning going live) for a blockchain-based system in the federal government.

Another key area of value is the ability to program automated data processing into the shared ledger based on a shared system of data governance using what are called smart contracts. Smart contracts were first introduced as a next level function on the Ethereum blockchain network. This went live in 2015 and serves as the second most prominent public blockchain after Bitcoin. The innovation of the Ethereum blockchain through the introduction of smart contracts was to allow for a variety of data processing to be programmed into the shared ledger. These could be created and modified for different types of data and use. This allowed the Ethereum blockchain network to be used as the foundation of a variety of new applications for blockchain in different industries, including supply chain, pharma and even art [2-1,2]. This smart contract functionality has been replicated and advanced in a number of different, newer blockchain platforms.

Cryptocurrency

At the core of the Bitcoin blockchain, value proposition is a utility for an independent electronic cash system that is independent of any government or banks. As a medium of exchange, it is trusted by unknown users across the network based on shared governance, mathematics and immutability of the distributed ledger. This shared trust and view of potential utility independent of a mistrusted banking system gave value to the bitcoins that were delivered to those who maintained and used the system. It may seem a bit circular at first, but the initial value of bitcoin was based on the potential of such a system. This closed system achieved real-world value on May 22, 2010, when one of the early users offered 10,000 bitcoins to anyone who would deliver or have delivered two pizzas to his home. The two Papa John's pizzas he received, ordered and paid for with dollars by another early user, may go down as one of the most expensive meals in history (at the time of this writing the value of those 10,000 Bitcoins is roughly $100 million.)

The philosophical and federal regulatory discussion of what is money, currency, store of value, etc. continues with respect to cryptocurrencies, from internet discussion boards, to books and classrooms, to the halls of the U.S. Congress. While it is a fascinating, critical and sometimes divisive conversation, it's not one we will be exploring here. Suffice to say that a large number of blockchains have been created as the foundation for coins, tokens and other units of exchange. Some of these have achieved notable market value either through early investments in the companies that created them or through the unique value—demonstrated or promised—in the application of those blockchains. This monetary value was, and is, a major driver in the research and development and adoption of blockchain solutions, but it is not the only area of value. We will explore some of these other areas of value in the pages ahead, including supply chain, healthcare and science.

The speed of transactions on a blockchain network has simultaneously critical limitations as well as rapidly advancing capabilities. Public blockchain financial transactions pale in comparison to systems such as credit cards for purchasing, contributing to the limitation on widespread use of cryptocurrency as day-to-day currency. For that reason, much work is going into new solutions to tackle this velocity issue in open networks. On the flip side, private and permissioned-access public systems can operate at a much higher velocity and volume given trade-offs to transparency and/or physical security.

This allows some of them to be competitive with legacy financial transaction systems, such as wire transfers when it comes to volume [2-3]. In addition, the distributed nature of the ledger of transactions involved significantly speeds up the check or remittance time for transactions, particularly across international borders where delays and associated cost of money transfer are significant. If you have ever waited days for a financial transfer or transaction to clear, you know the challenge. Much of this delay is based on waiting for the confirmation that funds are available and that they have been transferred in a way that can't be fraudulently exploited. Financial institutions around the world have begun to use blockchain systems for financial transfer, reducing the time window from days to seconds, hence saving money on fraud by shrinking that window. Sometimes they are even passing these savings along to the consumer.

The economics of blockchain coins and tokens has only begun to be explored in a new area of cryptoeconomics. The way these units are used, exchanged, increased and decreased in value as well as stabilized in a system, is being explored theoretically and in practice across open and closed systems. This area is critical to the understanding of how and where they might be utilized for the best value. The cryptoeconomics of medical research is an area too nebulous to be explored easily at this point, so it will not be a topic of this book. It will undoubtedly be a crucial area of study in the future.

Chapter 3

From Finance to Health: Way Beyond Bitcoin

Blockchain has been rapidly maturing first in finance and supply chain applications, but it is also developing a foothold across other industries. In healthcare, there are a variety of potential applications from purchasing to medical devices, to pharma supply chain where it has already shown real-world value and is quickly gaining traction. It is by looking at these that we can get a better sense of how and where this technology will begin to advance in application to health research.

Where Is It Useful?

As Bitcoin began demonstrating the value of such an automated trust system as a way of verifying financial transfers and transactions with no trusted third-party intermediary, people began to explore where similar applications of blockchain and related technology might be useful. The key to identifying potential use cases and industries was to see where this automated, or "trustless trust" as it was sometimes referred to, could bring value in itself or as a more rapid and cost-effective replacement for existing intermediaries. The boon of cryptocurrencies and initial coin offerings (ICOs) resulted in almost every industry being explored, but it was particularly the use cases and industries where trust was key, such as finance and medicine, that seemed ripe for exploration.

In addition to those areas in need of trust, the prospect of the speed and lower cost of auditing this technology could become another guide to where it might be applied. An audit is in some ways a verification of trust. This can take many forms, such as random auditing (like airport screening) when things are going relatively smooth in a certain setting, or it can be more directed when there is an example of a breakdown of trust (such as some Internal Revenue Service audits). The transactional ledger at the heart of blockchain becomes the auditor's best friend: immutable, accessible and containing all the relevant information if set up right.

Another setting where blockchain can bring benefit and where use cases were explored early was in systems that require different stakeholders to have different levels of access to information of the system. In many instances, this came from centralized offices that handed out the permissioned information or collected relevant information from the network when necessary. This can be a slow and costly process, especially when time is of the essence.

This process was the driver when Walmart began its groundbreaking blockchain pilots for food safety and product track and trace in case of a recall. Frequent food recalls in the case of outbreaks often affect the supplier and retailer who must immediately remove food that MIGHT be contaminated while awaiting more information on what specific subset of food is generating the problem based on its source.

In the case of Walmart's earliest successful pilot in the United States, it could take six days to identify the source of a package of sliced mangoes in a store [3-1]. If there were a contaminated batch from a specific source, it would be necessary to throw away all the produce since the source could not be determined for days. The pilot Walmart ran, putting information about each package throughout the entire supply chain on a blockchain to be accessed with appropriate permissions by each stakeholder, was hugely successful. It allowed a store manager or others at relevant supply chain stops to identify the suspect produce in seconds instead of days. Bad produce is removed, and good produce stays on the shelves. This saves money, and most importantly, this saves lives.

Supply Chain

The success Walmart has had with its pilots in food supply chain, with mangoes in the United States and pork in China, was just the beginning of a rapid expansion in piloting blockchain technology for supply chain.

Walmart joined a worldwide consortium including Dannon, Unilever, Dole, Driscoll's, Golden State Foods, Kroger, McCormick and Company, McLane Company, Nestlé, Tyson Foods and Unilever to continue exploring this technology for food supply chain efficiency and safety, multiplying the potential value of applications through collaboration and developing shared standards.

This interest in blockchain for food safety expanded to the government side as well. For example, Frank Yiannas, who went from blockchain skeptic to the head of the Walmart pilot, moved to the federal side in 2018 as Deputy Commissioner for food safety for the Food and Drug Administration (FDA). In early 2019, the FDA released a report highlighting the use of blockchain and other emerging technologies as the way forward for food safety for government and industry.

But the use of blockchain in supply chain goes beyond food safety. In 2016, the U.S. Department of Defense (DoD) began exploring the use of the technology for tracking airplane parts. The Department has gone on to award contracts to expand these capabilities to a new company called Simba Chain. This is in line with the expansion of use across the transportation industry, including a newly developed trade association, Blockchain in Transportation Association (BITA) [3-2].

The value to supply chain is rapidly transforming multiple industries from food to transportation. At its root, the value of blockchain is that *speed saves*: it saves money, and, in the case of health science, it saves lives. Those involved in the supply chain industry recognized the value blockchain brings to speeding up the ability to have the right information in the right hands, at the right time. It's as simple as that: When you know where everything is in a fast-moving supply chain, you can react quicker and in a more efficient manner when something needs to be found. Blockchain brings speed and granularity to this type of track and trace in several ways: it allows for peer-to-peer sharing of information in real time; it allows for automated entry and processing of the information from legacy systems via computer code known as smart contracts; in addition, it allows for permissioned access of this information from anywhere in the system as it is needed, rather than through a centralized office doing collation and processing only after a request is made.

The rapid acceptance advance and maturation of blockchain use in supply chain is a potential template for numerous other use cases. Several other systems could actually benefit from having one version of truth, trust, auditability and permissioned access to information. This could be an easy premade model for applying a distributed solution onto legacy systems across different industries to increase speed, quality and cost-effectiveness. In science, it helps to consider what is being tracked may not be a physical product, but instead information or data. Additionally, there may be secondary data or meta-data points critical for assessing that primary data. In food supply chain management, you might want to know the truck temperature for a delivery truck carrying ice cream. In science, for example, you may want to know the methodological data associated with an MRI data set being shared for research purposes (Figure 3.1, [3-3]).

This framework has led us to considering research data being processed into knowledge, and implemented into practice, akin to raw food being processed into refined product and used at a restaurant. Just as blockchain now allows us to track details about our food, its source, its quality and specifics about the shipping, we can do the same with research data, enabling us to separate "good data" from "bad data."

This verification of data is one of the factors that brought David Metcalf, Director, Mixed Emerging Technology Integration Lab (METIL) at University of Central Florida (UCF) Institute for Simulation and Training, to become interested in blockchain. He tells us that having more veracity in data will re-instill trust into the scientific community. A trust that is even more crucial

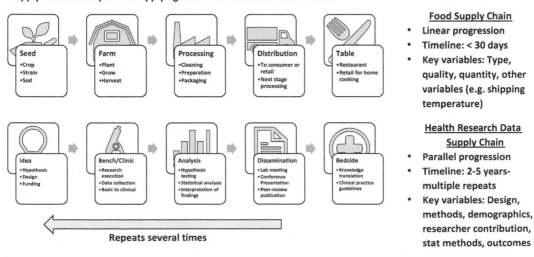

Farm to Table, Bench to Bedside: Health Research Data Supply Chain
Supply chain as template for applying blockchain to health research data

Figure 3.1   Farm to table, bench to bedside: an overview of the key elements in applying blockchain to supply chain track and trace and the parallels with health research data as a supply chain.

in the health science community—as with healthcare data "it can mean the difference between life and death."

"The trust has been lost because a lot of people have been doctoring data, making up studies in order to get tenure or fame. It takes years to prove that data is not true. In the midst of that, if you think of big studies funded by tobacco, pharma, etc. and you found that data is false, when you think about healthcare data, it has a cascading effect of consequences," David tells us.

This framework is still being shaped and advanced for supply chain, but with this comparison, we can begin to conceptualize how this technology can be utilized for research and other areas and begin to breakdown the distinctions and create new refined approaches.

Learning from existing use cases can extend beyond supply chain. Before we begin delving deeper into how blockchain can be used in health research, let's look at how it is being used across the healthcare field. Let's keep in mind that not only will there be other templates of use to learn from and build upon, but there is also the growing acceptance, comfort and capability building in healthcare that health research applications can align with. One—perhaps evident but still important—point is that pilots and use cases in healthcare with the most traction at the moment are the ones who will be able to lower costs: financial benefits are most of the times the catalyst for change.

David Houlding, Microsoft Principal Healthcare Lead and Chair of the Healthcare Information and Management Systems Society (HIMSS) Blockchain Healthcare Task Force, makes a point about this, telling us that when people start seeing blockchain's business value, it will be a watershed moment. "More healthcare organizations will use it, not because blockchain is cool, but because they get value from it," he tells us.

"The organizations trying to complete pilots and case studies will show what the business values are and what can be improved. Once we get to that point, it will establish a solid foothold for scale of delivery and use cases. It's fascinating. That's what could cause blockchain snowball in healthcare," David tells us.

Healthcare

The applications of blockchain in healthcare look like a microcosm of the use cases across different industries. After some early adopters started looking at applications in 2014–2015 (with a few even earlier), there was a consolidation of those early efforts in the 2016 U.S. Department of

Health & Human Services (HHS) Office of the National Coordinator blockchain for health and research white paper contest [3-4]. Fifteen winners were selected among the almost 70 different submissions ranging from insurance and billing applications, to electronic health records and health research applications. The winning selections came from government, academia and industry. The conference showcasing the winners was followed not long after by the first Distributed Health conference in the fall of 2016, which was the first industry showcase of its kind specific to blockchain and healthcare.

There was an expansion of interest following these events as practitioners in public and private health organizations sought to find useful applications for the technology, while both technologists and investors sought to explore this blockchain applications in the $8.5 trillion global health industry. As the ICO hype raged in 2017, several health-related currencies were launched, but largely this crypto-approach to healthcare did not catch on as much as elsewhere. One challenge was the robust and unique regulations relating to health information, health records and health research. Additional challenges associated notably with the sometimes messy world of health data also slowed the external interest.

Internally, health systems public and private, as well as a number of small companies better versed in health-related data than the average investor or fintech innovator continued the exploration. While hype still did emanate and attract more interest, there was a tempered realism in the blockchain and health community that lowered expectations. Different types of applications were at different levels of maturity and different stages of the Gartner Hype Cycle (which isn't actually a cycle, just a curve or wave, but people like it and it gets a lot of hype).

While discussing the key barriers to adoption in the healthcare field with Hyperledger's Behlendorf, he noted that part of it resides in education around blockchain, "because blockchain is associated with cryptos, how to make money fast etc."—one of the biggest misconceptions.

Part of the challenge, Brian says, is educating companies about the fact that there are ways to use blockchain without tokens, or proof of work, that can be about building network exchanges.

"You can track actors and see who the bad actors are and separate folks who are not. This improves outcomes. It's not just cutting costs out of bureaucracy but getting to resolution faster," he explains.

Let's now look at some of the key areas of applying blockchain to healthcare that have been developed along with some highlights as of the time of this writing:

Financial—Utilizing blockchain for financial applications in healthcare is in some ways similar to the fintech applications. It is relatively straightforward and is being explored by companies large and small. The billing and payment systems for private and public health systems have been very fractured and siloed, making it ripe for abuse, fraud and general confusion. The barriers to getting successful financial applications are not necessarily technical. The complexity of coding and billing data is one area that needs system knowledge and semantic solutions. The siloed and often non-transparent nature for healthcare organizations makes for an additional barrier, but one that lends value to blockchain applications that can create automated trust where there wasn't before across organizations.

There are several early efforts to creating solutions. Change Healthcare is a large U.S.-based health coverage organization that has gone all in to develop blockchain solutions and has begun primarily in the billing and payments area. They have acquired another small business leader in blockchain and healthcare, PokitDok, in late 2018 to enhance their efforts and seem to be out in front of their competitors.

Though it differs from some of the other early efforts, HHS blockchain-based Accelerate program for procurement has been one of the most high-profile and impactful early successes.

This program was developed in early 2018 as a way to bring more real-time buying power and savings to the 30,000 purchasers across the HHS system. Previously, purchasing information from five separate legacy systems was collected at a central set of offices. If a buyer wanted to know where to get the best value for a large purchase, say latex gloves for clinical use or statistical software for research, they would put in a request for strategic buying information from the central office information repository to find the best deal for the particular types of product and contract variables they had. This can be complex in the government purchasing system and would often take 4–5 months. Savings took time, and for this reason was sometimes not even sought or not received in a timely enough fashion to be valuable.

In early 2018, Jose Arrieta began as Acquisition Lead for HHS and spearheaded this government effort coming off of a successful pilot program at Government Services Administration where he had shown the power of blockchain to reduce the time and cost of vendor proposals by more than 90% each. Jose quickly developed a plan to streamline the sharing of acquisition information across the buyers in the HHS system. Utilizing a human design centered approach and engaging the buying stakeholders, he and his government and contractor support staff developed a blockchain-based system that layered across the existing five legacy systems. This processed the information already being input with a combination of machine learning to standardize the data and smart contracts to combine and process buyer-to-buyer shared information. Using a newly developed interface designed and tested with buyer input, the team was quickly able to give the 30,000 buyers real-time information on strategic buys that previously took months. Months to seconds with no added data input and a user-friendly interface that was rapidly adopted and utilized. This pilot was so successful that it quickly got federal approval to "go live" with an authority to operate (ATO) in late 2018 and is poised to give an 800%–1,000% return on investment (ROI) in its first full year of use when it is implemented in 2020 [3-5]. This will save the government and taxpayers tens of millions of dollars a year.

Jose tells us that the ATO was quickly approved because the business model improves security, moves to a cloud-based delivery model and redesigns business, which in turn allows to have visibility into multiple separate, disparate, siloed data sets and gives a flexible set of capabilities to rebuild the business by separating data and process. In other words, this approach lowers risk, modernizes the business mission and all that at a very low cost.

"What we've done with Accelerate is create an infrastructure. We proved we can index information, and separate aspects of the same story but that it can be analyzed separately so we can do deep learning and drive future outcomes. It could be applicable to any kind of data and research and how we went to market will create flexibility for government to replicate," he tells us.

Provider Directories and Credentialing—Another early healthcare use case that has demonstrated market value is the application of blockchain technology to the sharing and validation of information for provider directories and credentialing. The cost to upkeep records of providers with current and accurate information is significant across a variety of health and insurance systems. Even more costly in dollars and delays in providers being available to treat patients is the process of provider credentialing. Every time a doctor or nurse enters a new hospital or health system, and a regular interval within that system, these providers must have all of their information validated in order to treat patients. This can include records on education, past employment, references and malpractice history. The step is critical for hospitals to maintain quality care, but it is also costly, redundant and a major source of delay for bringing on new health providers who must wait through the months-long process before even seeing a patient.

Microsoft's Houlding explains that blockchain has an especially strong value proposition for directory use cases.

"Now, it's siloed across different healthcare organizations, it's redundant to maintain and the collective cost is too high. So, the opportunity is to put common data like common directories on a DLT, enabling updates to be rippled and eliminating inconsistencies, which causes delays in payments and issues that drives further costs," David tells us.

The recently formed Synaptic Health Alliance—a consortium of several major health-related companies, including Optum, Humana, UnitedHealth and Aetna/CVS—aims to explore where blockchain might be beneficial as a tool for sharing information across their systems with permissioned access and no one group holding all of the information. This group has focused on shared information for provider directories as their first pilot. Each company has their own list of network health providers and spends a lot of time and money on upkeep of the latest information. Many of the providers are in multiple networks. The group developed a shared, distributed system for keeping all of the provider information up-to-date and accurate. This allows them to combine resources to have shared savings, something that was not feasible from a business perspective with any one company "owning" the combined list. The shared information doesn't prevent continued competition in other areas but allows for cooperation to improve efficiency and quality for all the companies, providers and patients.

When it comes to the credentialing challenges, blockchain here too has begun demonstrating value as providing a layer of trust across multiple parties involved in requesting and providing information for this critical yet time-consuming and redundant process.

Microsoft's Houlding says that the way it's currently conducted creates a lot of redundant work. "Doctors have to be credentialed by organizations, who also verify if there are malpractice suits pending etc., and it has to be done every two years. So, by putting credentials on a blockchain, I can not only see them but also see who verified them. It delivers better healthcare at a better cost and it improves the experience of health professionals too, as they spend less time doing this."

ProCredEx (Professional Credentialing Exchange) and Hashed Health joined forces to create a blockchain-based architecture for a marketplace allowing the exchange and verification of the key information from the multiple independent sources involved. This has begun to attract users, including the Texas Health Care System, who can use this exchange to speed credentialing, reduce cost and redundancy and get trusted health providers to patients faster.

John Bass, Hashed Health CEO, tells us that the way he sees the value of blockchain is actually quite simple: it's its basic capability to solve issues around trust and transparency issues at the crux of the healthcare's system woes.

"The delivery of care is irrational in the U.S., mostly. The way we buy and sell healthcare is irrational. The current infrastructure and all our value chains focuses on enterprise and transaction and it's not sustainable. It's all too expensive and we're heading for a real crisis," John tells us.

But he adds that one way to fix these cost issues is to address that irrationality and the administrative burden, which manifests itself in various ways, whether in medical records, the pharma chain or clinical trials.

"There are real significant opportunities to improve efficiency by using distributed ledgers and blockchain to rethink how information flows through these ecosystems. Right now, we have a grand vision of how this will work in the future. At this point we need to stand way back and look at simple ways, at how some use cases prove value."

Medical Devices—There is growing interest in the potential for using blockchain with medical devices and the internet of medical things (IoMT). Both tracking akin to supply chain application, along with the potential for encryption to secure health related information has drawn this interest. One early pilot by Napier Edinburgh Napier University, Spiritus Partners and the National Health System (NHS) in Scotland show the value of blockchain to medical devices.

Previously, in hospitals across the NHS in Scotland, medical devices and associated training and adverse event information were tracked independently at each hospital. The locations of the devices were tracked centrally at a head office. Adverse event information, when something goes wrong with the device for a patient, was reported to the central office. When a significant problem with a device was assessed from these separate reports, guidance was sent from the central office to the hospital locations to stop the use of the device. This could take weeks, putting patients in jeopardy. Additionally, if devices moved around there might not be up-to-date information on where the devices are, or the training level of the staff that are using them.

The blockchain pilot enabled permissioned users at each hospital to see in real time where each device was located, and which staff were trained on them for use.

Susan Ramonat, Spiritus CEO, says that the ability to reduce cycle times up and down the supply chain during recalls or the ability of seeing patterns of events, across different geographies is exactly where DLTs add critical value.

"We are able to track a defibrillator implanted in Pennsylvania, to a patient who now has moved to Chicago for example. I will know that the patient has that implant, from that generation and it will also demonstrate physicians' contacts," Susan explains. This data flow and velocity are obviously crucial in case of a recall.

This enabled more rapid and effective sharing, transfer and trained use of the devices. More importantly, all adverse events for a device were tracked and visible across the system in real time with no delay. Along with this, staff and training levels associated with each use were tracked. If a threshold was reached, everyone on the system was able to be notified to stop or modify use based on the real-time information. This not only has the potential to save time, but it can also save lives.

Pharma Tracking and Supply Chain—In line with the rapid maturation of blockchain applications in industrial supply chain, the use in pharmaceutical supply chain is taking off. The FDA has approved two new pilots for this type of use. In one of the pilots, headed by Good Shepherd Pharmacy in Memphis, Tennessee, expensive drugs which were previously wasted, are now able to be re-introduced into the system. The goal is for the drugs to be used by those who could not otherwise afford them—something that makes sense when approximately 20% of the drugs that are manufactured are destroyed [3-6].

Expensive drugs for chemotherapy or rare diseases would often go to waste once they were given out for use if the assigned individual no longer needed them. There was no way to safely and appropriately get them back into the system. With blockchain, the non-profit pharmacy and its partners were able to re-introduce these drugs with an auditable tracking of their provenance, quality and authenticity that satisfied the regulators, providers and patients. This meant less waste and better treatment options for people in need. Phil Baker, Good Shepherd Pharmacy co-founder and CEO, and RemediChain co-founder, tells us that he chose to begin this pilot with chemotherapy drugs, as they're one of the most expensive and wasted prescriptions.

"In October 2018, we started accepting donated meds, we received $3 million of oral chemo equivalent in the first year and about $150,000 was redistributed," Phil says.

He adds that the chemo meds, is just the first use case, "the platform we're building will be able to recycle any kind of meds."

The other benefit of this pilot is that it will bring hard data around medication waste—data that can be used for research and inform manufacturers for example on how to reduce waste and create more efficient drugs. "And then there is the scale about the waste profiles, the waste trending data: if a drug is wasted 10 times more in Memphis, Tennessee compared to Buffalo, New York, it could help identify bad actors in the supply chain," Phil says.

Electronic Health Records—The holy grail of blockchain applications in healthcare seems to be the use for electronic medical records, cross-system interoperability and patient-centric control of your own records. The reason it is considered so important is that it would mark a transformation to a patient-centric health system allowing individuals to control the rights and access to their own medical data. There are several conceptual efforts and smaller real-world products and pilots working to achieve this, but there are also considerable barriers. The regulatory issues in the United States and abroad are major hurdles. Appropriate security and privacy to comply with laws relating to health information are a must for any application in this area. While it is the use case that attracts the most attention in healthcare, it also seems likely to be the one that will take the longest to realize, because of this major roadblock.

At the core of the use of blockchain for patient records and many other applications is the concept of self-sovereign identity, the unique digital identity assigned to each user or patient. This digital identity is necessary not only to align users with their records, but a fundamental aspect of allowing the patients themselves to control access to those records by providers, researchers, companies and others that may need to use the data. This gives the patients control and prevents exploitation of personal health information by third parties and the unauthorized selling of data.

Hyperledger's Behlendorf tells us that once regulatory concerns such as The Health Insurance Portability and Accountability Act (HIPAA) will be sorted out, his hope is that "in 20 years there will be a digital wallet with all my health records, with every prescription from every time I was on vacation for example, plus stuff I can add. Something I control and I can share, something I have access to and can revoke rights to. Blockchain will be essential to deliver this at scale and if we do nothing else but accomplish that, it'll be amazing."

Health Research—When it comes to health research, there is an array of applications that are being worked out. This will be the main focus of the last section of this book.

Chapter 4

Data Complexity

Blockchain's first mature adoption in the world of cryptocurrency was aided by the fact that there is already a straightforward and shared simplicity to the data and process in basic currency exchange. Other areas of potential tech application are more complex in their data and the processes involved in sharing and exchanging that data across users in a given network. How this complexity impacts application of blockchain technology and the trust and verification it can bring is only beginning to be explored.

3-D Blockchain Theory

In a short article about complexity levels of data relating to applications of blockchain to different use cases titled "3-D Blockchain Theory," the idea was stated [4-1]: "Increasingly complex dimensions of data used in a blockchain/distributed ledger will require increasingly complex consensus mechanisms to provide consistent and reliable governance across large enterprise systems."

This distinction is critical in considering how blockchain can be applied to health and health research data. Simply put, the applications that have worked in one type of industry or use case may not be as valuable or appropriate for use in systems with more complex data. Please keep in mind that this is untested as a universal theory at this point. That will come with time and more widespread applications across use cases and industry. The value of the concept comes in considering what, if anything, about healthcare and health research data may need to be taken into account when looking ahead to public blockchain uses for the data (Table 4.1).

Table 4.1 Data Complexity in Blockchain Use Cases

Complexity	Characteristics	Examples
First-level complexity: one-dimensional blockchain	Single variable (e.g., quantity) single fixed unit	Fintech, cryptocurrency
Second-level complexity: two-dimensional blockchain	Two variables (e.g., quantity and location) variable units	Supply chain
Third-level complexity: three-dimensional blockchain	Three + variables (e.g., quantity, type, reliability/confidence score) multiple units	Healthcare, research

The first layer of complexity, or one-dimensional (1-D) blockchain, relates to a single variable in a data set of the kind we see in pure financial blockchain applications like bitcoin (BTC) or ethereum (ETH). Here, a blockchain is a ledger of transactions of a single unit or partial unit (e.g., 0.33 BTC or 15 ETH). As noted in the original thesis, "Satoshi's elegant solution and its numerous protocol children are sufficient for firmly established consensus, and the transactional data has meaning independent of people or trusted third parties."

Most any governance protocol will suffice for this type of ledger. Trade-offs for speed, scaling and transparency will be more critical in selecting a governance protocol in this instance than the nature of the transactional data that is simply one variable or one dimension. This is what we can refer to as a 1-D blockchain.

The second level of complexity or second-dimensional (2-D) blockchain is one that captures transactional data of a two-variable nature. This is commonly seen in supply chain for example. Transaction data contains not only quantity of a unit or partial unit but also a second variable relating to the type of unit (e.g., 6 rods, 13 widgets, 9 rods + 5 widgets). At this point, most blockchains or distributed ledgers with this type of data are closed or permissioned blockchains, rather than widely used public applications. The consensus mechanisms for a widely used public or open blockchain of this type may need a specific type or modification of traditional consensus mechanisms.

The third level of complexity or three-dimensional (3-D) blockchain would then have three discrete variables involved. In this case, transactions may record quantity, type and some level-of-evidence equivalency

(5 neurocognitive assessment scores from a randomized controlled trial, 630 blood pressure measurements from medical records, 33 functional magnetic resonance imaging (fMRIs) from an observational study, etc.). A public 3-D blockchain like this does not yet exist and may not even have many post-pilot private blockchain equivalents. Nonetheless, the concept is critical to begin to understand what this might look like for healthcare and health research information, as well as to understand what impact this might have on consensus mechanism selection.

What this all means is that there seems to be potential challenges with the types and complexities of data transactions that are captured via block-chain. How this verification would occur and what consensus mechanisms would be useful and valid, or at least perform the best, may still need to be worked out.

This isn't to say that this dimensional blockchain theory must be true, but there seems to be sufficient basis for treating these different data sets in unique ways as we begin to consider what it would mean to have confirmation by consensus of any transactions associated with this data.

Metcalf, at the Institute for Simulation and Training, tells us that thanks to blockchain, we could have much better data that can be used across multiple research organizations and populations, which in turn would lead to faster and more reliable data, the ability to get drugs to market quicker and have a better validity and verification that they can do no harm and work as advertised.

"This would lead to life and cost savings. It would also re-instill some trust in government regulators, big pharma, in groups and organizations that get paid to do these studies. The whole ecosystem," David notes.

Health and Research Data

Healthcare data is messy. Health information is collected by a variety of people in a variety of locations in all sorts of different ways. Think about just a simple bit of health information, such as blood pressure (bp). A simple reading of systolic over diastolic, 120/80 for example. Now think of all of the different situations that data might be collected: at home with a store bought bp monitor after 30 minutes of relaxing, at the machine in the pharmacy after 30 minutes in traffic, at the doctor's office after a morning fast, at a minute clinic after a burger and fries, at the hospital while under anesthesia for surgery and in the park via Fitbit during a long run.

This is the same kind of information—systolic over diastolic—but all representing different states of a person's physiology and bp, recorded by different devices of different validity and accuracy, under different types of supervision from self-report to readings captured by a medical professional. The data represents different things. Even the trends of each (where repeatable) are different. Now consider where all of this data is stored. Is it mergeable? Would you want to merge it? Would there be any value in that? Maybe if you had a lot of associated meta-data (time of day, activity, recent diet, etc.), but without that it may just be noise. And what about the formatting of the data? If you were to bring it all together in an excel sheet, would each cell match or would there need to be reformatting to even make it readable or workable? There are a lot of questions and variables for just a simple health data point like blood pressure from one person. So how much more complicated can large amounts of health data be and how can we make it more streamlined, secure and transparent.

Health data is often complex, messy and unorganized. The messiness is sometimes not apparent when looking at data from hundreds of thousands of individuals in aggregate. Any volume of data can be crunched into statistical programs for some sort of result, and the sheer volume can mean it would look significant. What is unseen, unless you are familiar with the data, where it comes from, and the variance involved is just what data can be coupled, merged and combined; and with what caveats.

The complexity of health data becomes even more complicated when you begin to bring in coding elements such as International Classification of Disease (ICD) codes as ways the health data is recorded, bundled and tracked. These codes have been established to give different entities from providers to insurance companies, the ability to standardize health data relating to different diseases, injuries and conditions. The codes themselves are numerous, and often the standards of use by different disciplines of providers specializing in different areas can also vary greatly. For example, with traumatic brain injury (TBI), there are myriad different ways a post-injury headache can be recorded depending on who saw the patient, in what setting, at what time point and with what background information.

There are standards for health information, but these are general guidelines that leave a wide amount of interpretation. The challenges of the data are something that needs to be considered not only for end-use considerations—with respect to data science and even artificial intelligence and machine learning—but also from the outset with any application of blockchain. For example, the types of standards that can best be utilized and how to get compliance will be a critical challenge of any blockchain related to clinical data.

Other challenges to think about include the types of platforms, governance protocols and platforms that work best depending on the particular use case, the nature of the blockchain (private vs. public) as well as the users themselves.

When talking to Heather Leigh Flannery, CEO of ConsenSys Health, she notes that one of the barriers to adoption is the compliance ambiguity in areas of policy and regulation across jurisdictions around the world.

"The immaturity of technical standards and the absence of any certification to conformity to standards don't exist, because the standards don't exist," Heather says. She notes that the fear of vendor lock in and the issue of what platform, whether they interoperate and at what levels, is a real problem for healthcare "as people have PTSD about what's happened with electronic health records (EHRs)."

"The paradigm is moving forward—people are super concerned that they will have a lock in with a set of vendors who will become the next Amazon, Apple, Facebook, and they're worried about that."

When it comes to research data, the situation is both better and worse. Research studies tend to be much more specific in how the data is collected and recorded. Each study has its own protocol that could lend itself to much of the detail for standards needed in developing a related blockchain protocol. At the same time, the data between studies, even on the same health issue, is often not aligned and mergeable. And given the stringent researcher and regulatory standards, there is not necessarily a lot of flexibility in how the data may be adjusted to match a different study. Further, there is limited research utility in general health data. Large amounts of health data are great for answering general questions and refining knowledge to more specific questions to be asked of formal research, but because of the messy nature of the health data, not a lot of actionable conclusions can be drawn. This is why clinical practice guidelines are drawn only from higher levels of evidence.

As we saw earlier, the volume of information available from EHRs does not necessarily translate into actionable evidence on the level required for standard clinical practice guidance. There is too much variability and noise in the system to draw definitive conclusions from health data. Research on this data by way of health data science doesn't get you there either. There is sometimes a lack of understanding about just what is required evidence to support changing clinical practice. Data science or big data doesn't cut it. You need more refined and advanced research.

Dealing with Complexity

One of the ways to begin preparing standards for the use of health and research data in blockchain and develop a system that can help inform clinical practice is to create new standards, building from existing standards, for the data. This goes beyond just technical or formatting standards, which are already being addressed by the Fast Healthcare Interoperability Standards (FHIR standards) in healthcare. The focus needs to be on data standards at a much more granular level.

To get to this level of standards, it will be necessary to differentiate between data collected in different health research areas. Standards set up for cardiology research and practice may not necessarily fit the bill when it comes to neurology. Gastroenterology is not oncology, and so on. Data standards by discipline and sub-discipline will be the necessary level of meticulous detail to expand use of blockchain for health and research.

Chapter 5

Blockchain Is People

Blockchain isn't just a new technology. Yes, its technical aspects are critical, but it is much more than that. Blockchain is a technical layer to our integrated digital world that allows a complete restructuring of how we share and track data. How we trust that data. And how we verify that trust. Blockchain at its root is people. People across a network agreeing to a shared governance of how data in a system will be shared, processed and accessed. People creating and agreeing to utilize a computer protocol that captures that governance in code and layers of smart contracts.

Dr. Alex Cahana, ConsenSys Health Chief Medical Officer, likes to put it this way: "In general, my one liner is that blockchain is the solution to the social issue of trust. We live in a world where I want to trust everything, but I just can't."

"By virtue of decentralization and by coding rules of behavior, it adds a certainty to the trustworthiness of the transaction," Alex says.

Col. John Boyd made a very pertinent comment about the importance of things in a distributed network: "People, ideas, things, in that order." Ahead of his time in many respects, this thought seems like a foundation of how blockchain can most successfully be used, especially in a complex system like science and knowledge generation (Figure 5.1). People make up the network that utilizes data and its outputs; ideas are the governance protocols that underlies how this data is to be captured, processed, accessed and shared; and things are the tech that makes up the blockchain network. This order is important. In a simple 1-D system like finance, you may be able to capture a pre-existing idea in a blockchain and convince a network to use

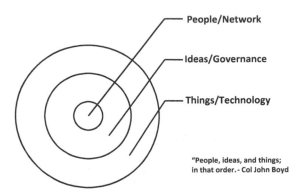

Figure 5.1 People, ideas and things: framework of how people/nodes in the block-chain network are the foundation, with the shared ideas are captured in the governance, and then incorporated into the tech thing that creates the interface.

it through utility, innovation or blunt force sales. When it comes to complex 2-D and 3-D systems, you are much more likely to be successful and add a mission of market value if you own or create the network first and then build a system based on governance developed with their input or the input of representatives they trust.

Network

Users are critical for the success and value of any blockchain. Bitcoin would have no value if there weren't millions of people who were willing to host and run the program and trade monetary value to buy in at this point. They have all agreed to the standards built into the system, the governance designed and coded into the protocol. Similarly, every blockchain application must have users to be of value: users who have bought into the system and agreed to the governance. These individuals understand the value that it brings and the problem that it solves.

In designing and running a blockchain system, there are experts or representatives that design, host and maintain that system. As mentioned earlier, Bitcoin was designed by a person or persons known as Satoshi Nakamoto. Its ledger is hosted on every node that buys in and downloads the ledger, and it is maintained by a small cadre of dedicated volunteers. Those who maintain it is fully decentralized like to handwave past this fact, but so far, every system has some centralization: the question is how much is tolerable for the trade-offs.

In blockchain application for healthcare and research, this balance is likely to look much different, especially in the early stages. Experts or representatives who understand the system represented and the data involved will play a role in designing, creating and maintaining any distributed system. It is those people and their view of the world, and how it translates to the governance, that must be trusted.

John Bass of Hashed Health has noted in an article [5-1] that any blockchain without a network is just an expensive academic exercise. This is very true. A governance system that people don't wish to trust to use, is not worth much more than a self-licking ice cream cone. It has no wider purpose or validity.

Whether you design a blockchain alone, with a small group, or with the representation of those you hope will be the network of users will be critical to the success of the effort. The buy-in is key, and you either must force compliance by owning the network, convince those involved to begin using it through negotiation, marketing or influence, or else you must include those individuals or representatives involved in the design of the system itself.

Protocol

No blockchain will advance without standards for the data. Standards for what each recorded transaction represents and how it is formatted and recorded. Financial standards are relatively easy, with the 1-D exchange of a unit (i.e., a Bitcoin or Satoshi) being what is recorded with each transaction. With more advanced 2-D, 3-D and beyond, there will be a more complex set of standards and representation of the data involved. In some cases, the data can be flattened (3-D represented as 2-D data), but the key is that there are standards.

For health and research, there are many standards to lean on, but the data is rich enough that not all of these will be sufficient for all use cases. Many applications of blockchain in health and research will require new or more robust standards. These can be designed by a single person or small group, but this may not be sufficient to get it accepted by the network of users it needs for implementation.

These standards, what they represent and how the data they represent are exchanged is the next factor. A financial unit is exchanged, and the transaction validated in a simple financial blockchain governance structure.

How more complex data is represented, handled and exchanged is a question of governance that must be answered for each application. With smart contracts and automated processing of the data, there will be a greater need for agreed-upon governance of the system.

When it comes to governance, ConsenSys Health's Flannery tells us that it's also a major issue in healthcare and life science.

"We got decent at governance as a civilization, but this is governance of something else—something shared and mutualized between x number of parties and institutions. The method of governing is not clear; when we talk about governance in this context, it's different than corporate governance, that template doesn't fit."

The protocol is the digital representative of the shared or agreed-upon governance. It is the coding that captures the standards and automated processing into the tech. How this is done depends upon the design and those involved, whether it is the use of a preformed system with the flexibility to be adapted to different uses, modification of a malleable platform to create a richer system or a boutique system designed specifically for the use case at hand.

Platform

In selecting, modifying or creating a platform, considering the users involved becomes a critical first juncture. Whether you own the network and wish to get compliance and alignment to current operations or want to build a new system aligning with your network of users' needs, a human design centered approach is critical. Including the users in the design to describe the problem area and needs will be more likely to ensure usefulness and value.

There is a wide array of existing platforms and an infinite numbers or possible designs for any particular use case. These will offer different advantages and trade-offs in speed, scale, transparency, security and convenience among other things. By assessing the needs of the use case and the network, by considering the input of those users through the human centered design approach, you will be able to select the ideal platform for your use case.

Every system needs to be tested before it is road ready. The more complex the use case, the more it will take back and forth with the users to ensure it is ready for use. Given the value of what may be contained, including health information, it is important to test the system not only from a user perspective but from a bad actor perspective as well. This iterative process will expose the flaws and harden the system before use.

SCIENCE IS EASY

Science seems complex but broken into its fundamental parts is easier to understand.

Chapter 6

Good Science

Science gives us a better understanding of the world, the knowledge to create new medical devices and find new ways to treat diseases. For those who are not directly involved in scientific research, it is sometimes viewed as a highly complex process. In reality, while the technical details have become increasingly complex, the basic process is simple. What science is, where it is practiced and how it impacts our lives are starting points for understanding how we can get more from our investment in science.

History of Science

Science is the systematic study of the natural world, everything around us and within. Science started with human curiosity and developed through stages into the systematic process we know today. It gives us the foundational building blocks of human knowledge and captures a snapshot of the most accurate representation of our reality that we can describe at this time.

Science is not perfect, but like Churchill's take on democracy "it is the worst form except for all the other forms that have been tried from time to time." So, what is science the worst (except for all of the others) at doing? Predicting. Science is about not simply categorizing and describing the world around us, though this is a key part. It is also about using that information to predict what will happen next (Figure 6.1).

The scientific process as is most commonly used today was formalized by Sir Francis Bacon. It makes up the foundation of how we

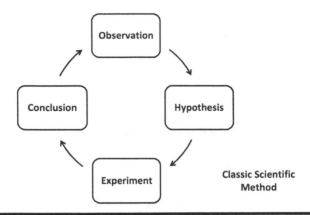

Figure 6.1 Scientific method: the key steps in the scientific process are (a) observation, (b) hypothesis, (c) experiment and (d) conclusion.

practice science. At its core, it is simple: Observe, hypothesize, test, conclude. Let's look at a simple example. We'll revisit this example in more detail throughout the book.

- **Observe**—A child notices that she and her friends get taller as they get older.
- **Hypothesize**—General hypothesis: People get taller as they get older. More specific hypothesis: People grow one inch per year.
- **Experiment**—Measure everyone in a school class one year and then the next. The results show that every student has grown, but not exactly one inch (except one kid) or even the same amount.
- **Conclude**—People get taller as they get older (hypothesis confirmed) and people do not grow 1 inch per year (hypothesis rejected).

You can immediately ask, what about the teacher, older individuals, people with abnormal growth patterns, people in other places, people in other times, etc.? This identifies not the limits of science, but some of the limits to generalizability of specific findings and the importance of sampling.

The basis of experimental science practiced around the world is basically the same. There are other key elements as you get into the weeds of execution: studying what has previously been discovered, complex methodology and statistics, interpretation of findings, peer-reviewed reporting and more. We'll touch on these more as we move forward. For now, this is the foundation of science as we explore how it impacts us in sickness and in health, along with where it can be improved in its current execution.

Scientific Process

Many people do science. You might be applying the scientific method if you observe that different ways of driving to work take different amounts of time, hypothesize one way is fastest, time yourself each way and conclude if your guess was right or wrong. For the purposes of this book, we'll be focusing on those people doing science for the purpose of reporting their findings into the general body of scientific knowledge.

The main role of science is performed by the principal investigator, or PI, of a study. This is the person who has the ultimate responsibility for the design, execution, integrity and findings of the study; along with the associated ethics and legal responsibility. The PI might work alone, though that is exceedingly rare these days. More often the PI has co-investigators, associate investigators, research coordinators, research associates, research assistants and people in specialty roles from research technicians to grants and writing assistants. In academic circles, undergraduate students, graduate students, post-doctoral fellows and sometimes medical students also contribute significantly to research.

Most health research is done by private industry in the United States (70%) and around the world (60%) [6-1]. This research is often targeted at specific problems and applications. While the process is scientific, often the findings of private research are only reported internally rather than publicly in the overall body of scientific knowledge. Some general findings from private research may be published, or more specific findings after delay in order to realize the monetary value before sharing. Negative findings from private research are rarely published.

Government also funds and executes science across the world. Some of the government run science—particularly in the military—may be limited in the same proprietary or closed reporting way as private research. Despite this, governmental research contributes a significant portion of the overall body of scientific literature.

Academic institutions contribute to execution and funding of research as well. In many instances, academic researchers are involved in executing research funded by government and/or private organizations. Academic institutions contribute the bulk of scientific literature. In this setting, peer-reviewed publications have taken on an economy of their own, along with an imperative. Publish or perish.

Non-governmental organizations also contribute to research funding and execution. Examples of this include professional societies and disease-specific charities.

Let's take a look at how all of these things—method, people, organizations—come together for a generic research study. We'll focus on medical research.

1. PI and Co-PIs have an idea based on their knowledge of existing literature and clinical observations.
2. They write a proposal and develop a research design with a specific set of hypotheses and plan to test them.
3. This proposal is submitted for funding. Once funding is received, the proposal is drafted into a research protocol.
4. The protocol receives regulatory review and approval from an institutional review board (IRB).
5. The study is executed by the research team, and data is gathered from patients or existing databases as governed by the protocol.
6. The data is analyzed by the research team and conclusions are drawn by senior researchers based on knowledge of current literature.
7. These findings are presented in internal and/or professional meetings for review and feedback. Internal reports on the initial findings may be drafted. This information is referred to as "gray literature."
8. The refined findings are submitted to a medical/science journal for peer-review and publication.

Benefits of Science

The overall benefit of science, sometimes lost in the short term, is to build humanity's body of knowledge; finding by finding, brick by brick. Sometimes the bricks crumble or need to be replaced. Often new findings raise new questions and open the opportunity for more observations, studies and findings.

In the long term, this iterative process of scientific discovery, confirmation and correction gives us the foundation of knowledge to provide evidence and direction for practical application. These can be concrete applications such as engineered products and devices, or they can be abstract knowledge applications such as processes or treatments.

The application of science, developed as engineering or in health as medicine, is the concrete, short-term goal of most requirement-driven research. This is where the phrase "research & development" (R&D) comes from. We'll dive further into the R&D process in health and medicine in later chapters.

Suffice to say that this is the reason for most research funding. It is critical to note that regardless of the goal of the funding, the discoveries and reports/papers themselves contribute to the overall body of scientific knowledge. Science builds on science.

In addition, science has the benefit of being a major economic driver in the United States and around the world. R&D is a $1.7 trillion annual industry worldwide [6-2]. There are millions of people employed directly or in support of scientific research. This role as an economic driver is most often cited in discussions of investment value of research funding. While it may seem to be a secondary benefit to the goals of science, from an economic perspective, it is the ROI most easily tracked. Other aspects of science ROI are challenging due to the difficulty in relating attribution to specific research dollars and the challenge of tracking those dollars across the years and decades it can take to influence policy or practice that generates positive economic impact. We'll look more at these aspects of research ROI in later chapters.

Chapter 7

Evidence-Based Medicine

Scientific research provides us with the evidence on which much of our new medical treatments are based. The medicine is only as good as the evidence. The process of knowledge creation and then translating it into medicine takes time and requires many gateways to be cleared as the evidence is gathered to support changes in medical practice.

Bench to Bedside

The process of taking new biomedical ideas and turning them into evidence-based medical practice is sometimes referred to as going from "bench to bedside." This encompasses several iterations of the research process as new knowledge is created and refined. Then, there is a process by which this knowledge is aligned with existing knowledge of best practices. This latter stage is sometimes known as knowledge translation. Application of new knowledge is as critical and sometimes as unstructured as the research and creation of new knowledge that feeds into it. Some ideas can enter into the bench to bedside timeline midway, and there are multiple intersecting efforts across any one scientific field or area of exploration.

The general process consists of a new idea, concept or insight being developed and tested in basic research. This is done in the context of previous research and published findings. The results of these experiments are reported in professional society meetings and conferences, or other pre-publication reports that constitute what is referred to as "gray literature." The scientific community in that field provides feedback.

Once refined by this feedback, the findings are submitted to an appropriate journal for peer-review, further feedback and refinement, and eventually publication. These peer-reviewed journals in a field make up the longitudinal record or ledger of scientific knowledge in that field. Each manuscript is recorded, vetted and able to be referenced by future work which builds upon it.

As evidence builds to support an insight or treatment in the basic scientific literature, it may gain prominence to those looking to translate new insights into clinical application. A series of phases of clinical trial allows for the methodical and safe progression of testing the safety, efficacy and effectiveness of new treatments in humans. But a major issue is that this iterative series of science is more heavily regulated and significantly more expensive than basic research. Here, ideas for new treatments are evaluated to increase the evidence base that will point toward and allow for the widespread and recommended use of the treatment in clinical practice. This process can take years, and often can include ideas that come not only from basic research but also from clinical observation and observational research studies. There are many paths for new ideas, though the confluence of these eventually comes at the later phases of clinical trials and development of clinical recommendations and clinical practice guidelines (CPGs).

CPGs are the medical industry standard for incorporating health research findings into straightforward guidance for healthcare providers who treat patients. These are created by groups of experts in a particular health issue coming together and going over the latest findings in the field that meet specific criteria for scientific evidence. These findings are generally limited to peer-reviewed publications from recognized journals describing the results of randomized controlled trials, formal systematic reviews of the literature meta-analyses of combined study data. Other types of research findings such as basic research, case studies, observational studies and cohort studies may inform CPG development indirectly by being the precursor or included in the studies that are considered, but they generally aren't looked at directly.

It's important to note that there is often a gap between the health research studies we hear about in the news and those included in directly advancing guidance for medical providers who treat patients. For example, a story in the news might be a new clinical research finding reported at a professional conference; it might not have yet gone through the informal and formal vetting of peer researchers; or it may represent only a piece of evidence that needs to be incorporated into the whole field of study. And sometimes it is basic research that is anticipated to potentially impact clinical care but is a long way off from actually contributing directly. One could think about it akin to building a new deck or wing of a house: Just finding the potentially right parts and even having those parts delivered does not equal the careful construction of some sturdy new part of the house, ready for use.

This patient pace of process does serve a critical function. Just as you wouldn't want to have a home renovation project thrown together with piles of materials and no blueprint or eye toward sturdiness and safety, you don't want to change clinical care on a whim with each new announcement of a research finding. The caution is to carefully evaluate each new piece of evidence for quality and fit it into the overall structure that currently exists for treatment. Advances in treatment come with an appropriate evidence-based foundation, and major changes to treatment should only come after a significant review and support that it will not only be helpful but will not be one step forward and two steps back.

It takes 17 years on average to go from bench to bedside. This means that almost two decades passes from the early exploration of an idea to its confirmation as part of the clinical treatment options. This timeline is moving forward simultaneously for a variety of potential treatments for any given health issue at any given time, with periodic reviews and assessments of what information is out there that deserves inclusion in informing new treatments. Most of this time is spent on iterative research studies happening somewhat independently, with information from these aligning at each step along the way to form the foundation of future research. Eventually, when enough evidence has accumulated, there is support for changing practice. A significant amount of the pre-research administrative time is spent preparing this research, seeking funding, getting regulatory approvals. After the formal research is conducted, it takes time to analyze and report these findings, publish them with feedback, and for these findings to make their way into the overall reviews that inform care. Much of this time spent is critical to quality, but parts can be sped up. The bottom line is that it doesn't much matter when you are waiting for improvements in care for you or a loved one. And the question is, can we do better? This is where blockchain and other emerging technologies can come into play, and play a critical role in speeding up processes (Figure 7.1).

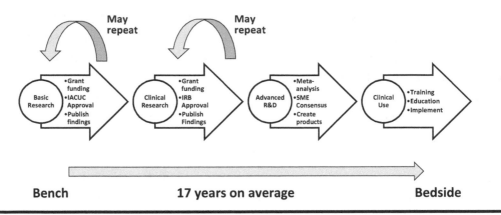

Figure 7.1 Bench to bedside: this is the general timeline for a new treatment idea to be tested and eventually incorporated into standard clinical practice if it is worthwhile. This takes on average 17 years, though it can vary considerably.

In "Enhancing Federal Research: Traumatic Brain Injury and Blockchain Technology 1.5," [7-1] the question was asked:

> What if we could speed up science, improve the quality for fewer wrong turns and wasted effort, and reduce the overall cost of execution improving the ROI of research? What if we could give more time, better quality of life and more chance of long-term reprieve to those families dealing with cancer? What if we could improve the quality of life and outcomes for the veteran with traumatic brain injury (TBI) and his spouse and three kids? What if we could extend the time a university professor with Alzheimer's could continue to teach our kids and enjoy time with her husband?
>
> What if we could cure childhood disease allowing kids to grow up, achieve their dreams, and change the world? It takes on average 17 years to get from idea to treatment in health science research. Imagine you have a 1-year old daughter diagnosed with a disease. There is no cure, no treatment, and no current research on the sickness. Even if there's a research-ready idea, it could take until her 18th birthday to be put into practice. Maybe you have millions of dollars to throw at research to speed this up a year or two. Maybe you can get her into a clinical trial (with some risk) a few years earlier. But it would still take into her teenage years before there is hope, and a potential end to the suffering.

To shorten this time, it is necessary to dissect it to get a better understanding of which parts are necessary, which may be redundant, where it can be sped up and how it can be better coordinated and aligned. [University] researcher Zoe Slote Morris and her colleagues have described the delays in the article, "The answer is 17 years, what is the question: understanding time lags in translational research." Dr. Morris and her colleagues describe the areas of delay including grant awards, ethical approvals, publication, phase I, II, III trials, approvals for drugs, post-marketing testing and guideline preparation, along with the repetition and time lag involved in each.

Here are some of those steps along the timeline to give you a better sense of what is taking up the time for the advancement of medicine to occur. First, there is often years of foundation of basic biomedical research, the kind that happens in labs with cell cultures and animal models, to inform the general field of knowledge and highlight certain approaches to new treatments that may align with viable clinical treatments to improve outcomes in human patients. There is some disagreement on the value and ethics (i.e., stem cells and animal testing) of certain types of this pre-clinical basic research. The bottom line is that it has contributed to major advancements in human knowledge and medicine, and also that it is highly inefficient for a variety of reasons, some of which we will consider later in this book.

Other ideas for new clinical treatments may come from observation by health providers during clinical care (often referred to as case studies) or through more formal observation studies or retrospective studies of medical records. These all advance medical knowledge and contribute to the body of peer-reviewed medical literature that advances the field. Again, there are inefficiencies that can be improved upon in how this information is processed, combined, compared and ultimately used in the next level of support for the advancement of treatment in a particular health area.

Once an idea has come together enough that researchers want to try it in a human population to see how it works, there becomes a more formal series of steps that takes place to get the funding, set up the study, get the necessary regulatory approvals, conduct the study, analyze the data, report the results and have this piece of knowledge incorporated into the broader knowledge for that particular field. Sometimes this happens only once before the evidence is strong enough to contribute more substantively towards the development of new clinical practice. Other times, there will be a series of consecutive studies to get there. This is particularly true when there is a new pharmaceutical, medical device or invasive treatment as the earlier rounds are focused more on safety and efficacy, with the later rounds focused on how well it works to make people better.

Conducting a clinical research study, including recruiting and consenting patients, delivering the treatment and gathering the initial data, gathering follow-up data (often for months to years after the initial treatment), analyzing and interpreting the results, and writing them up for communication and incorporating feedback can usually take 3–5 years or more. Besides the research itself, here are some of the steps involved:

Idea and hypothesis—The ideas that make up the hypotheses in science aren't available in a pre-order catalog, they come from a spark usually rooted in years or decades of knowledge gathering from the published literature and refined in the lab or clinic doing related research. The individuals generating these ideas need to compare them against other findings that have been tried and reported in the peer-reviewed literature that is the record of science, as well as any potential ongoing work. Knowledge of the ongoing work takes interactions with the science community and tracking new ideas being presented at conferences pre-publication along with other locations. There is a lack of reporting of negative results, results that don't demonstrate potential effectiveness of a given treatment in a trial or experiment, which makes evaluating new ideas against already tried ideas even more difficult. There is a lot of room for improving this, by speeding up how the accumulated knowledge can be shared, for example.

Research development and design—Before even applying for funding, getting regulatory approval, and starting a study, research must be meticulously designed and checked for soundness, statistical validity, ethical approach to patient engagement, appropriate resources and a variety of other areas. Data gathering, storage, access, usage and analyses must all be laid out in advance.

Grant preparation—In order to get funding to conduct the study, researchers have to often competitively apply for grants from external or internal funding sources. These can be public or private, and usually will take months to prepare, especially for the more competitive funding sources like the National Institutes of Health.

This consists of putting your ideas into an extensive and specific format in the context of other previous done work in the field to be evaluated by experts. This has a high level of administrative detail as the entire study must be outlined for evaluation, including all regulatory considerations, data management and governance, along with budgetary details. This is costly and time consuming to complete. Many universities have multiple adminis-trative offices to assist researchers and assure compliance with internal and external policies. The cost of this administrative infrastructure is then passed on to the funding agencies as overhead or indirect costs that can sometimes exceed 50% of the cost of the research itself. Many of the steps involved in the process are redundant, both the internal systems and the systems uti-lized by the external funders. This means that if a researcher doesn't get selected for funding in a particular opportunity, they have to take many of the same time consuming and costly steps again. With selection for funding sometimes lower than 10% for the more competitive processes, this means a lot of time and money goes into just the administratively costs around researchers trying to get funding, and organizations whose mission it is to advance medicine spending significant amounts on the administrative pro-cesses involved in accepting applications for funding. Blockchain—and DLT in general—may be able to help here too by eliminating redundancies and lowering costs.

Grant review and selection—This is the process the funding agency goes through to have experts evaluate the applications and determine which research will be funded. It is a critical step, yet takes many months to coordinate in most cases, and may still contain significant amounts of bias toward known entities, such as established organizations and research-ers with longer track records, and bias toward selection of safe, incremental research. This may be what is desired in some cases, but in many others dif-fers in practice to what the funding agencies outline as their goal.

Regulatory approval—Regulatory approval is one of the most challenging areas for many researchers. For clinical research, it requires ethical approval of an Institutional Review Board (IRB) that ensures it aligns with the many federal laws and standards for conducting clinical research. These are gov-erned by the U.S. Department of Health & Human Services (HHS) Office of Civil Rights and are the result of a great many past abuses of patients for research (e.g., Tuskeegee Experiments) [7-2]. The rules ensure ethical research conduct that respects both patient safety and patient privacy.

These are a few of the research-related activities that can take consider-able time and effort with each iterative round of research [7-3]. We'll explore more later on how these areas can slow the progress of research and how things might be improved and sped up, without losing the quality and integ-rity these processes require.

In general, most medical treatments will not see widespread recommen-dation and implementation unless they have gone through the gauntlet of clinical trials, have attained enough evidence to support their use and have met certain criteria for regulatory approval. In some instances, this can vary from country to country, creating an environment for "medical tourism" where people seek treatments they can't get in the United States in less regulated environments. In some cases, this can end badly, with distinct impact differing based on approved/non-approved status of treatments (i.e., the immunomodulatory drug thalidomide in Europe and the United States) [7-4]. The trade-offs between what is safe and allowed, and what is available can sometimes be frustrating for those in need of treatment now as the slow process of science moves forward. On a population level, the caution makes sense, but on an individual level, it results in suffering and dying when a chance at improvement or cure is worth the risk. This trade-off has been recognized in recent "right to try legislation."

If a person has cancer or other potentially deadly or debilitating disease, they might be tempted to try new or experimental procedures. This can sometimes lead to improvements in outcomes beyond what exists in standard care, but it can also result in false hope and even potentially worsening the problem with an untested treatment. In the United States, this is tightly regulated, but it is less controlled in other parts of the world, generating the so-called medical tourism. This can lead to unfortunate choices by desperate people. Treatments that haven't been shown to be effective in recognized research may provide useful, but they may also be ineffective or even treatments pushed by those that wish to exploit the desperate population.

Medical Evidence

Once a threshold of medical evidence has been reached for something to be promoted for use in regular clinical treatment, there is no magic signal that alerts all providers and makes it the standard. In some cases, there is not even a clear threshold of evidence before it is recognized as ready. There are regulatory safety and efficacy standards that need to be reached—such as the ones set by the Food and Drug Administration (FDA)—but each new treatment is still competing against several others across multiple health systems, hospitals and care centers, as well as providers who make the recommendations and decisions for patients relating to care.

The latter stages of knowledge translation, and the implementation of new clinical practice in medicine are as complex as the development of the evidence supporting it through research. In some cases, public or private health systems may make recommendations for treatment beyond or in advance or more formal standards or guidelines to fill gaps in knowledge. In other instances, individual providers, with widely varying levels of experience and knowledge of the latest findings, may prefer very different treatment for the same patient. Different fields of medicine can differ on their degree of standardization as well. Some like cardiology have made considerable strides toward developing key objective standards for diagnosis and subsequent guidelines for treatment. Other fields like mental or psychological health are very far from anything approaching standard treatment in many cases.

A major factor in treatment decision making can also be cost of treatment. This can come up whether the patient is covered by private insurance or public coverage, and certainly when there is no cost coverage at all. In the United States, insurance coverage or federal program coverage for a particular treatment doesn't come into place automatically simply because doctors have decided it works best. There is a series of evaluations, reviews of evidence and standard reports required before a treatment is covered. In some cases, this can take years, with the use of the treatment as an "off-label" use becoming common place before it is approved as supported by the evidence if the treatment is cheap enough. If it is prohibitively expensive treatment, this is less likely and sometimes serves as a point of resistance to coverage of the treatment. A couple of examples of this illustrate the challenges.

Based on some anecdotal evidence and preliminary studies, from the mid-2000s to the early 2010s, there was some evidence to support the use of a common generic drug, methylphenidate, to improve chances of recovery in patients with severe brain injuries and who were in a coma. Because of the low cost of the drug, minimal side effect impact on unconscious patients and lack of other options, the use of this treatment was relatively common among doctors familiar with the treatment. At the same time, randomized controlled trials—the gold standard for clinical research evidence—were not able to recruit enough patients for trials (with family members consenting to their involvement) to deliver sufficient evidence to make this an approved practice. It was unethical of the doctors not to inform the family that the treatment was already used "off-label." This often led families to opt for the off-label use rather than enrolling in a study where their loved one only had a 50% chance of getting the real drug vs. a placebo. On an individual level, this made sense, but prevented patients from being recruited for the study (where they might get the placebo). Therefore, they couldn't complete the study and without it there was insufficient evidence for the treatment to be approved for widespread use.

A different case where concerns with costs delayed the implementation of a treatment was in the late 2000s, with the use of cognitive rehabilitation for mild TBI with persistent issues after six months. In many cases of mild TBI, people get better with rest and minimal treatment in a short period of time. In a small number of cases, issues with cognitive problems along with other physiological issues like balance problems and headaches can persist for months or years. When these problems are chronic it can be very disruptive for the people involved. Treatments in this area were of particular interest for the military. There was ample evidence supporting the potential for cognitive rehabilitation to help similar problems in people recovering from more serious brain injury, but there was not a solid body of evidence to support the effective use in mild TBI cases, especially given that the cognitive rehabilitation treatments were time consuming (many hours over several weeks) and costly due to the need for specialists who weren't available everywhere. Adding to the confusion was that there was no standard on what these treatments looked like specifically, and some of the only evidence was in a civilian population rather than a military population where health problems and effectiveness of treatments can differ.

There was enough push from patient advocates to cover these treatments that Congress got involved and directed the DoD in 2010 to conduct a randomized controlled study on cog rehab for Service members with mild TBI with persistent symptoms and determine whether there was sufficient evidence to justify coverage. It took several years to design, approve, recruit, conduct and analyze a study that provided this evidence, but in 2011, the Study of Cognitive Rehabilitation Effectiveness (SCORE) trial at the San Antonio Military Medical Center delivered. Several more rapid, more expensive studies were also commissioned, but these fell short of the necessary requirements and evidence, often being completed in a civilian population or not completed at all.

In the end, there was sufficient evidence from the SCORE trial to have it incorporated into the new CPGs for mild TBI, but the treatment was still not approved for coverage under TRICARE, the military's insurance plan, because the Pentagon officials did not think sufficient levels of insurance type review had occurred to justify it. It was only once it was clarified that civilian insurance coverage reviews had approved the treatment that the recommendation went forward to Congress that it should be covered.

CPGs represent a key milestone in the advancement of research on new treatment translated into new knowledge to be implemented in day-to-day clinical care. They are developed through consensus of the top minds in the field, based on the shared review of the strongest evidence research in the field has produced. They are periodically reviewed and updated to ensure the guidance will inform the best treatment based on the evidence.

Different hospitals and health systems may develop their own CPGs to inform best practices for their patient population. Professional societies and non-profit groups may also develop their own to be disseminated and help advance treatment in the health area where they are focused. In some cases, organizations may opt to develop guidance on a topic that falls short of or is merely a precursor to a CPG. In the case of the DoD, these are referred to as Clinical Recommendations. The goal of these partial measures is to provide some of the best guidance possible in an area where the top standards of evidence don't yet exist. These are then largely used to offer a starting point for those who may not be well-versed in the literature or their own experience with a problem, rather than to standardize practice on the best approach. These clinical recommendations can also serve as the foundation for data gathering and research on the effectiveness of different approaches.

Levels of Evidence

Experts have characterized and ranked the different types of medical and scientific evidence that can inform new treatments and evidence-based medicine. Roughly speaking these are individual observation or anecdote, case report, expert opinion, observational studies, cohort studies, controlled trials, randomized controlled trials (RCT) and systematic meta-analyses. This order presents (from lowest to highest) the weight and reliability of the evidence in considering a body of evidence for new recommending and approving new treatments (Figure 7.2).

At the upper end of the pyramid, relatively fewer cases, with much more standardized, controlled and structured data is required to achieve the level of evidence required for considering or rejecting a treatment. The cumulative impact of one level at the upper end (i.e., RCT) may supersede the next level (i.e., meta-analyses) as the multiple trials effectively add up to the impact of the next level of evidence.

Conversely, the lower levels of evidence rarely can accumulate to have the impact of the layers above. The reason for this is often summed up

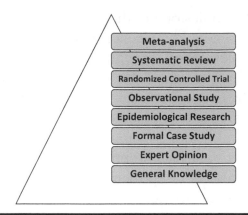

Figure 7.2   Levels of evidence pyramid: this is the general progression of reliability of clinical evidence to contribute to clinical practice. Lower levels are more abundant but better for refining questions and defining new studies. Upper levels are generally required to support wide adoption in clinical practice.

with the adage, "the plural of anecdote is not evidence." Simply put, lack of standardization, or even information about the respective methodology of data gathering for each individual case, prevents the accumulation from ever achieving necessary statistical power and significance to be relied upon as strong evidence. Instead, these layers are valuable places of observation that can point to where researchers may want to look next with a more structured trial for potential treatments.

There has been a tremendous increase in ability and focus on big data approaches to analyzing health-related information. This has value for potential insight but is also sometimes overly relied upon for generating the evidence for best practices. The challenge is that if there has been no effort to standardize the data collection, and insufficient information about the respective methodology of each data point, there are too many unknown variables to draw actionable conclusions. Big data is often a good place to start to look for trends and begin asking key questions. This allows for more targeted hypotheses to be tested in advanced research.

Chapter 8

Science Crisis

Science is a highly trusted professional field. Its hundreds of years of history has produced new knowledge that is the foundation of many technological and medical advances. There are also significant issues with science that are sometimes below the radar. From reproducibility issues to significant back-logs and delays, there are a number of areas relating to research that can be improved. By understanding these issues, we understand how much more valuable science can be and how blockchain and DLT can help.

Reproducibility Issues

Science is the testing of hypotheses against real world or experimental data. It's also determining whether what you think is the case is objectively supported by the data. This is done with sufficient data to make the results statistically significant and powerful enough to draw conclusions. How you conducted the experiment, collected the data and did the analysis should be captured in enough detail to be able to be repeated by the same group or another group, and get the same general results. This sets up the standard for replicability (repeated by the same group) and reproducibility (repeated by another group). The idea that research is reproducible is what makes it considered to be generalizable, worth reporting to the world, and the foundation or partial foundation for action. In the world of medicine, this translates to the research that underlies our evidence-based medicine being expected to be reproducible enough to serve as the foundation for how we make decisions of life or death in the treatments given to patients by medical professionals.

Unfortunately, that is not always the case. Science has a reproducibility crisis.

A 2015 study by Freedman et al. demonstrated that nearly $30 billion in basic research, or 20% of the $150 billion dollars in biomedical research in the United States each year, is not reproducible [8-1]. That's one in five studies that provides the foundation for life and death treatment decisions that is not reproducible, and therefore shouldn't be fit for general consumption in the scientific literature and by the medical community. In some areas of health research, the numbers are much worse. For example, some areas of psychology have been found to be 50%–70% NOT reproducible [8-2]. This means there are some sub-sectors of health research that are more noise than signal, more false than true and story than science. This false information then contributes to not only how we see the world of health and medicine but also how we make critical decisions about treatment. Evidence-based medicine based on bad evidence is bad medicine.

Where does this tainted research come from and why isn't it a bigger issue? These are reasonable and crucial questions to ask. The basis is rarely outright fraud. Only a tiny fraction of papers is retracted, stemming from people falsifying data, which can have tremendous impacts as we'll see in a bit. Most of the time, the reasons underlying irreproducible research include sloppy science, poor reporting of methods, bad equipment or materials, or the biases of the researchers themselves. Science has in many ways scaled past the careful practice of its modern founding and appears to have lost some quality in the process.

Through the early 1900s, science was often done from end to end by small groups or single individuals. These people had often devoted their lives to the pursuit of knowledge and understanding the universe around us. There was not necessarily even for the promotion of the public good and was usually pretty distant from any career development or profit motive. Science was frequently a monastic endeavor. The current system was designed around this curiosity motive, with professional societies and systems like the modern peer review developing around it. Status and competition began to play an increasing role, but science was still frequently an almost separate society with its own motives and goals. The role science played in the applied engineering was growing, but still limited.

It was post-World War II that we saw a recognition of the value of scientific research to rapidly drive economic progress and innovation.

This scientific–industrial partnership expanded rapidly in the United States based on some of the successful, rapid applications of science in the recent war, most notably the Manhattan Project and the development and deployment of the first atomic bomb. It was also driven by the work of Vannevar Bush who captured these successful processes into a vision of what could be achieved both economically and scientifically if federal resources continued to be devoted scientific research. This spawned federal efforts like the National Science Foundation along with a great number of academic and industry-based efforts to expand research and development.

Many of these early scientific renaissance projects continued to focus on defense-based developments and their civilian offshoots. This military industrial drive was constantly fueled by the Cold War competition between the United States and its Western allies with the Soviet Union, including the subsequent space race. While defense, weapons, transportation and exploration led the early expansion of science, rapid expansion of health-focused research was not far behind. The budget for the newly named National Institutes of Health (NIH) jumped dramatically from its precursor immediately post-World War II and continued to see exponential growth for the next few decades. This pushed forward both basic research into how human health and disease developed as well as more direct applications of medicine to treat disease.

This expansion in both the physical and biomedical sciences was done in large part in partnership with universities where the traditional systems of scientific careers and checks and balances were still in play. Professional societies, conference presentations, peer-review and academic tenure were the standards and remain so today. This expanded interest and funding of research has caused these institutional standards to become somewhat misaligned with their origins as primarily focused on truth, consensus and constant correction. As numbers of new researchers swelled but positions for tenure stayed flat and often occupied longer by a healthier population of incumbents, fewer students went through the same trajectory. Publish or perish, became the metric-based rallying cry, and science became more of what it measured in the form of published papers, but less of what it was supposed to seek in the form of truth.

Wendy Charles, PhD, BurstIQ Chief Scientific Officer, puts it this way: "We think about science as involving ethical, independent and objective studies. But science is never truly objective. It's not objective in the way studies are designed, funding is obtained, results are written for publication, or the peer-review process is done at academic journals."

Wendy notes that research is very expensive, but funding opportunities are highly competitive, a problem compounded by the fact that granting agencies tend to fund research that is popular (and safe) instead of research that is novel or controversial.

"There is a publish or perish approach in many universities. This causes scientists to publish quickly and superficially instead of taking the time to thoroughly explore an issue and create depth of understanding," she adds.

This discrepancy has not been caused by any one factor, but it becomes clear things have fallen out of balance. We have seen a massive expansion in graduate students, post-docs, journals, publications, funding, overhead costs and administration while the tenure track positions have shrunk to just 15% or less of science PhDs. This means more graduate students competing for fewer tenure track positions that they are being trained for. It means extended periods of highly skilled but low pay as post-docs continue this competition for years, often becoming "perma-docs" or untenured assistant research faculty. Throughout this process, those individuals being trained and functioning in a system setup for lifelong employment as end-to-end scientific research investigators are increasingly incentivized by short-term goals to reach the next rung of the ladder. The increasing number of high paying options outside of academic science is also attractive to those who may have more career-minded goals and less attention to the meticulous details science requires. Without intent, many of these rushed, stressed, underpaid contributors with misaligned incentive to science and knowledge building in general can make up the bulk of the sloppy science that contributes to these horrible rates of 20% or more findings lacking reproducibility.

How bad is 20% bad biomedical science, really? Imagine 20% of the groceries you have delivered turns out to be rotten. Imagine one in five of your paychecks bounces. Is it a problem? Of course, it is, and you would act accordingly. Because of the delay in identification of bad science, we may not have the same instinctive reaction, but the situation is actually worse. In science, every new finding is predicated on the body of knowledge, captured in the literature, that came before it. This ever-growing body of accepted peer-reviewed literature is the forever record of science on which new research can be done without having to replicate every study that came before. Bad science that gets entered into the system of trust in the scientific literature can take years or decades to be identified and removed, if it is detected in the first place. Bad science can continue to infect everything that comes after it, sometimes without anyone realizing it.

If we had something tainted like this in the food supply chain, it would be identified relatively quickly once people were getting sick or dying and tracked back to the source to be corrected. During the period of unknown, products of unknown quality would be ordered to be pulled from the shelves until the source of the problem could be traced and identified, allowing safety to be restored. The system might not be perfect, but we see this frequently in e-coli outbreaks that result in food recalls or even suspension of use and sale of a particular type of product like lettuce or strawberries. In biomedical science, there is no such recall system. Because of the extended timelines for the supply chain of research data being years long, it is much harder to detect problems and track them back to the source. Science relies on the integrity of the researchers and the limited checks of the peer-reviewed system to keep the quality and reproducibility high. It also relies on the slow decades-long process of correction to weed out problems and correct our movement toward more accurate and actionable knowledge.

If food is making us sick, we have a system to track, trace and correct the problem. Medicines that we take have a similar system if recall is needed, along with a robust regulatory system before the public is even exposed to them. Neither of these is perfect, but both are light years ahead of any system in science. In science we rely much more heavily on trust. As we have begun to realize, in its current configuration, there is a significant likelihood that the trust is misplaced, and we lack a system of rapid detection and correction. We are careful to the point of frustrating delays in regulating the medicines we put into our bodies, but we have far fewer quality controls on the evidence that underlies that same evidence-based medicine.

One example of just how hard bad science is to detect much less fix, even in the case of outright fraud is the recent case of a prominent cardiology researcher that was fired from Harvard after it was identified that he had been falsifying critical research for 15 years [8-3]. Despite the first warning signs coming more than a decade earlier, the slow process of verification and correction plodded along as this bad science continued to be disseminated and acted upon. The groundbreaking cardiac stem cell research became the standard knowledge of the field. Therapies were developed based on the bad research, funding decisions were made based on how well new research aligned with the bad findings, and for more than a decade clinical decisions were made in the context of this bad research and everything that followed. How many people were given useless treatment instead of something that might have helped? How many opportunities for new findings were lost because they didn't align with the bad research?

The real and opportunity cost of this bad science, at one of the most premier U.S. research facilities and published in some of the most premier journals, are hard to fathom. Yet it barely made the news.

A much more widely known impact of bad science, though often not attributed to the scientific community, is the inaccurate connection between measles, mumps and rubella (MMR) vaccine and autism. A now retracted study published in the journal *Lancet* in 1998 pointed to a connection between the common MMR vaccine and autism. Despite the study being of a small number of children (12) the impact was significant, helping to fuel a still active anti-vax community pushing back on vaccinations based in no small part on this research [8-4]. The study was called into question when it was learned that the children had been specifically selected based on pre-existing conditions, their parents' assessment of an association between the onset of symptoms and the vaccine and several open lawsuits by those families against the vaccine manufacturers. It took 12 years for *Lancet* to retract the article despite these issues being raised in the years immediately following the study. In that timeframe, millions were spent on research that failed to verify the specious claims. More importantly, thousands of children were impacted by measles outbreaks fueled by fear of vaccines, and desperation of parents with children affected by autism looking for a reason and being duped by bad science.

This bad science not only impedes progress, diverts resources and slows down the advancement of new treatments and better outcomes, but it can also have detrimental health outcomes. The majority of the 20% of bad biomedical science isn't even noticed and simply becomes noise in the system at best or directly infects future research and resources in the wrong direction. Like inefficient fuel for a car, this bad science slows our progress toward new, actionable knowledge.

17 Years—Bench to Bedside

The quality breakdown is not the only delay in medical science. The long process to go from bench to bedside, or new idea to trusted treatment, takes 17 years. Much of this is time is critical to test hypotheses and verify outcomes, but there are a number of areas that could be sped up without loss of quality. While we must be respectful of the necessary processes and safeguards, we should also be willing to identify and call out those areas that are unnecessary delays due to redundancy, inefficiency, siloing and bureaucratic overreach.

First let's have a closer look at the timeline and then a deeper dive on some of the areas of delays. Here is a highly generalized overview of a clinical research study:

1. **Idea Generation (Indeterminant; days to years)**—New ideas are developed based on a combination of education, observation, research practice, community engagement and literature reading and review; ideas can come suddenly or through a slow, deliberative process. This portion of a clinical study is generally preceded by earlier basic research, research on retrospective clinical data or other precursor research in years prior.

2. **Research Design (1–3 months)**—Ideas are formed into hypotheses and research to test these is designed based on previously published studies and in the context of available resources and partnerships. The design itself can usually be accomplished in a few months, often as part of the application for funding, though the gathering of partners and incorporation of colleague feedback can often be spread out over a much longer period in a "measure twice, design once" sort of way.

3. **Funding (6–12 months)**—Applications for funding can take a few months to develop (see design above), but also take several months to be reviewed and selected or rejected along with other applicants. This time consists of a variety of steps including internal administrative signoff by the applicant's institution, administrative processing by the funding institution, subject matter expert review to inform the funding selection, and notification and coordination of funding distribution.

4. **Regulatory Approval (2–4 months)**—Before any work can begin, a study must receive regulatory approval from its institutional review board (IRB) along with second-level review where appropriate and any IRB approval by partner organization. The coordination between these reviews for multi-site studies can become very challenging as changes requested to the research protocol by one IRB need to then be approved by the partner IRBs. Regulatory approval can frequently be the source of much more extensive delays.

5. **Research Data Collection (1–3 years)**—This is the execution of the research protocol as designed, including recruiting patients for the study, conducting the treatment or observation, collecting data and following up for additional data collection as needed. Length of studies can vary widely based on the number of patients needed for the study,

the number of patients of the correct criteria available and willing to participate, and the timeframe of the follow-ups.

6. **Analysis and Interpretation (2–3 months)**—This is the statistical analysis outlined in the research protocol on the data that has been collected. Sometimes there can be interim analyses at set time points during the study as well as at the end.

7. **Interpretation (1–2 months)**—The results of these analyses are then interpreted by the senior researchers and other select colleagues in the context of study conditions and previous findings to draw conclusions to report as findings.

8. **Dissemination and Publishing (6–12 months)**—The findings from the research are reported in different forums from internal lab meetings to professional conferences. This can take the form of poster presentations or platform presentations focused only on the study, or as the latest findings at the end of a more robust foundational presentation. The purpose is to expose the findings and conclusions to the community to solicit feedback prior to formal preparation of a manuscript to be submitted for publication in a peer-reviewed journal.

This whole process takes a few years and is generally repeated in iterative cycles of advanced studies and more conclusion findings with each cycle. This iterative decade or more of clinical research is book ended on the front end by years of similar but often shorter cycled basic research to form the foundation or the clinical observation, case study write up and sometimes retrospective data analysis of available clinical data. Each of these precursor steps can contain some or all of the same steps and associated delays of the core clinical research. On the back end of the bench to bedside timeline as the research findings are incorporated into the literature is the steps of more comprehensive replication studies, meta-analyses and systematic reviews to determine if the appropriate levels of evidence have been met to incorporate the findings into newly formed or update clinical guidance based on expert consensus.

Research Delays

Many of the delay periods that could stand to be improved are in the early phases before the research begins. These are largely administrative delays caused by redundancy and bottlenecks in the approval of research on a grand scale. The process itself is still of value, it is simply not being executed with anything approaching efficiency. As there are generally several cycles of research on the way from bench to bedside, these delay periods can be compounded. Here are a few of the key areas of delay:

Grant Review—Administrative and subject matter review time are a cause of many of the delays in the progress from bench to bedside. While some of these may be with good reason (administrative checks for completeness, subject matter working groups for appropriateness and scientific merit), these processes have become extended and frequently redundant, with an emphasis placed on administrative convenience over rapid facilitation of selecting the best science for funding.

Let's assume a researcher has an idea for a new treatment and wishes to seek funding to test this in a clinical research study. The researcher would identify a funding target, perhaps a federal agency, and begin to develop a proposal to apply for the funding. This proposal would include the basic study design including statistical analyses, along with background on the problem area and the proposed idea, putting it into context of the literature for the reviewer. This proposal would also include the details on the key collaborators and the study team, the facilities, budget and a great many other details about the organization the research belongs to that would be receiving the funds.

As the researcher is preparing all of this, many parallel steps for signoff on the proposal have to take place within the university. These include organization assurance, regulatory and budgetary signoff, along with letters of collaboration or support from external partners, who often have to get similar approvals from their own organizations. This has to happen every time a new funding proposal goes in, even if that proposal wasn't accepted and is being resubmitted. The process is highly detailed, very time consuming and laborious, and contains high levels of redundancy. That said the universities charge the funding agencies a high premium for administrative overhead to cover the costs of this and have found that multiple intermediary offices are the best way to handle the process of many researchers applying for grants.

At the funding agency, there is a parallel series of administrative checks to ensure each submission contains all of the dozens of parts and signoffs required before the proposal is vetted for content. Incomplete submissions are in most cases rejected, making administrative detail rather than innovation or impact of the idea the first vetting principal. Universities with a highly developed administrative program tend to have this process most well-oiled to meet the appropriate criteria, giving them a leg up on getting more research funding, including the administrative overhead costs that can be an additional 50% or on top of the basic funding amount.

At the funding agency, the critical step of subject matter review then takes place. Lead and secondary reviewers for each proposal pore over all of the substantive detail and independently score the proposals. These reviewers come together for review sessions where they present, discuss and prioritize the proposals. Here, reviewers become advocates for those they feel are worthy of support. Usually, an overall comparative score is developed and ranking of the proposal for funding purposes occurs. This is a critical step in the objective review and selection of proposals to be funded. There may not be much of it that can be sped up, though there has been some concern with bias creeping into the process as it has become bigger, with those who have previously gotten funding becoming the presumptive favorite for future funding. The downside to this is that it may ensure a race to the safe middle at the expense of more innovative proposals from newer researchers and smaller universities.

Regulatory—Regulatory review and oversight of clinical research plays a crucial role in the safety and privacy of patients. With that in mind there may be areas where better communication, document tracking and auditability would be helpful for both the regulators and speeding the process up for the researchers. Benefits to this would be better safety and privacy along with faster research. Win-win. Some areas of redundancy, especially with multi-site trials, are multiple IRBs. Centralized IRBs may be a benefit, while coordinated decentralized IRBs may be even better.

Publication review—Publication review, peer-review, is a critical component of successful science. It is a mechanism for screening out or helping to refine sub-par science from the forever record. Without it, science would be as impactful at creating new knowledge as the op-ed section of the paper. The model used for this has not undergone significant update for decades or centuries. A couple of fairly well-established scientists (associate professor level) who volunteer their time to review and provide feedback is the standard. With this model now significantly scaled, several problems have arisen. In addition to bias issues, including some relating to competition, there has been a critical issue with delays in peer-review compared to the rapid pace of everything else. Are there places for improvement while preserving quality?

As Helen Disney, CEO of London-based blockchain education and events blockchain platform Unblocked Events, notes, "Scientists have some frustration with existing scientific review processes because certain processes are embedded in academia and to get funding you have to follow a certain process, like being published in peer-reviewed journals. But there are barriers to entry with seniority, etc."

Disney adds that the problem is compounded by the fact that there is a lot of waste: of time, money and people doing the same research over and over again. "So one of the things blockchain can do is allow people to be recognized in a more granular way for what they do: if they can document their research on a blockchain, then it's time stamped and immutable and other people could openly access that piece of knowledge for the good of society. Not for the good of an organization. It's a different way of doing scientific research, but it opens lots of possibilities for knowledge sharing in a less weighted process than we have now."

While no one profession or organization is to blame for these delays or be said to directly benefit, it is useful to understand who is deriving indirect benefits from the extended process. This will help us understand where there might be some resistance to the prospect of speeding things up.

Chapter 9

Open Science

The struggle in the scientific community with some of the shortcomings of science, coupled with the desire to make science more open and effective, has paved the way for the Open Science framework, which has begun to take shape over the past couple of decades. Theoretically, this framework can resolve many of these issues, but in reality, it has been slow to take hold. Looking at some of the successes of Open Science, as well as some of the barriers, can make it more feasible to chart a course for more realistic progress and identify how new technological tools may help this along.

Foundations

Open Science is the idea that research, especially publicly funded research, should be open and transparent, and the results should be freely available. There are several layers of achievable Open Science from a practical stand-point, having to do with funding and who is covering the costs of publish-ing. While these ideas have been developing for a couple of decades and have gained some traction, existing systems and organizations have not all—yet—fully or even partially bought into the entire spectrum of Open Science. Karmen Condic-Jurkic, PhD, explains the need for Open Science this way: "Science is a global effort in the end. As a scientist, I use work from all over the world. Open Science says science is a publicly funded endeavor so it should be publicly available."

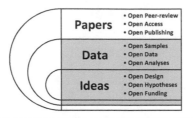

Papers	• Open Peer-review • Open Access • Open Publishing
Data	• Open Samples • Open Data • Open Analyses
Ideas	• Open Design • Open Hypotheses • Open Funding

Figure 9.1   Open Science: a diagram of the main areas and sub-areas involved in the discussion and application of Open Science.

The goals of Open Science are transparency and openness on all aspects of research to avoid fraud and allow peer scrutiny; and to allow for open access for anyone to publish their findings and availability of these to all (Figure 9.1).

Open Science operations can be found in a variety of non-profit organizations established over the past couple of decades and a variety of more nascent grass roots movement across many fields of science. Many non-profit groups committed to the goals. Some publishers and pre-publishers devoted to some aspects (fee to publish common to cover costs). Other publishers have made some nods to open access, including hybrid journals that allow for both open access and paywalled content. Other journals have become all open access, such as Frontiers, while still operating a for-profit model that includes author processing charges (APCs). APCs are also found in various not-for-profit organizations like Public Library of Science (PLoS).

Successes

Sharing ideas about research in the early stages has some seen some widespread adoption in line with the Open Science goals. The pre-funded ideas and hypotheses are harder to share without the originators getting scooped on the opportunities for funding by faster and better equipped labs. The successes have mostly been in sharing the concepts of already funded studies.

Another key place this has been achieved on a widespread basis is with the required submission of U.S. federally funded clinical research study overviews to a single website, clinicaltrials.gov. Here, others can review ongoing funded studies to see what has been funded, understand the basic approaches currently underway and avoid simultaneous duplication without methodological alignment, unless that is the desired goal. While the site is an indicator of some success for the Open Science goals with respect to federal funding, it has also been limited due to partial compliance by federally funded researchers.

Sharing findings and study results has become ubiquitous at the level of abstract overviews, at least in the biomedical sciences. PubMed is a federally funded repository that allows anyone to see and search abstracts from all the published literature. This is made freely available to the public. The ability to read all the details in a full manuscript is still often limited. Some publishers always make their full papers freely available. Others do not. A requirement from the federal government has given a timeframe after which all federally funded research publications must be fully and freely available.

There are several examples where shared databases are available for other researchers to utilize. Federal Interagency Traumatic Brain Injury Research (FITBIR) system has aligned common research data elements and mandated their use in federally funded traumatic brain injury (TBI) research to allow for merging of multiple data sets with higher quality results in related meta-analyses due to data standardization. This site is the result of almost a decade's worth of work by representatives from the DoD, U.S. Department of Veterans Affairs and U.S. Department of Health and Human Services, plus experts across academia and industry. Common data elements were selected to be the standard for all federally funded TBI research to facilitate meta-analyses of studies using a shared centralized database. The success in establishing the system have been somewhat undercut by researchers unwilling to share their data before they have had a chance to publish key findings from it. At issue is the worry that they might be scooped by other labs before they can realize the professional benefits of publishing the results of their data.

University of Michigan manages shared, freely available data sets as a service for those federally funded entities that wish to share their data to the broader research community. Federal agency research programs such as the Army Study to Assess Risk and Resilience in Servicemembers (Army STARRS) program make their data sets available through the University of Michigan for anyone to use presuming they have the appropriate resources and expertise, plus an IRB-approved protocol to do the research.

Yauheni Solad, MD, MHS—Medical Director, Digital Health and Telemedicine, Yale New Haven Health, tells us that "blockchain can allow researchers to use the same public research hopefully, which will help us get much better information about what are we truly analyzing and what are we producing. So, it can first, help us have a validation point, and second, create an infrastructure that will simplify open data sharing."

Barriers

The biggest barrier to Open Science is that scientists are afraid of getting scooped: by not sharing their data, some think they will maintain an edge. Sharing ideas runs the risk of someone using it to get funding before you. Sharing data or results runs the risk of someone publishing or gleaning insight before you have achieved this value. The system has developed around a much different paradigm than Open Science. While many or even most scientists might be on board with the idea in theory, in practice until the system and incentives change, there will be a lack of will to move toward this theory in reality.

Publishers represent another barrier to major progress by the Open Science movement. Many publishers, including the most revered and sought after, are for-profit and still utilize a business model of paid access along with paid submission in some cases. Top-tier journals such as *Cell*, *Nature* and *Science* are included here. The competition to publish in these top-tier journals outstrips any desire to move an Open Science agenda forward in the scientific community. These types of publications make careers as those who publish there are more likely to be noticed for grants, accolades and tenure. The way this dynamic has developed is both fascinating as well as seedy. There was an open manipulation of the scientific ethos that underlie the development and rapid expansion of the current publishing structure [9-1].

There has certainly been a move toward open access over the past two decades in the publishing industry. But the prominence of big journals and impact factors as criteria for funding and career have prevented wider use. There are some more comprehensive plans to shift the system toward open access such as Plan S in Europe. The buy-in for these projects is still limited but gaining wider adoption [9-2]. There are still remaining questions about what any unintended consequences might be to such legislation.

ConsenSys Health's Cahana shares a few of his thoughts on these barriers to adoption, which he thinks are mostly driven by human nature.

"People are greedy, jealous, stupid. It's clear that there are [healthcare] stakeholders whose business models will be more impacted than others in a decentralized economy, so they're anxious," Alex tells us. He further suggests that instead of looking at barriers, we look at how can we facilitate adoption. "Stop saying 'de-intermediation' and talk about 'reintermediation' For example, even if I hate banks they won't go away. Instead of praying to the gods of burning banks, let's look at what is in the banking economy that can be improved? It's about leveraging the technology, about re-intermediation, bringing on value to valueless intermediaries. Blockchain adoption is evolutionary, it's not an all or nothing phenomenon. Technologists understand that so they can create agile solutions. Don't be dogmatic."

The second thing, he says, is that we should think about collaborative cooptation, not competition.

"It's all about creating networks of knowledge."

Cahana's third and perhaps most crucial point is that the soft belly of blockchain lies in the fundamental difference between having things right and doing the right thing.

"There's no magic in a distributed ledger, all it does is that it tries to create a game or an economic environment where it's a lot harder to be a bad actor and it encourages good actors to continue to do what they do. It's all about trying to do the right thing. We don't have to find a nebulous middle between free and controlled markets, we have to transition from free to open market: free means everyone is free to join, producers, counter producers, non-producers. An open market is opened only to producers. And that's what blockchain is: zero tolerance for bad players."

Bureaucracy may be the most significant factor in the barriers to wider acceptance of the Open Science movement. These can create delays in making data sets available, as universities attempt to control access and findings to maintain a hold on any intellectual property involved. Even in managed systems, or internal systems, there are many signoffs required and subsequent delays in access. The administrative overhead the universities charge, sometimes 50% on top of the basic amount of grant funding, is another driver to maintain the status quo. Without these administrative funds, there might need to be cutbacks at the university level. This disincentives movement toward an Open Science system.

THE DAO OF SCIENCE

A distributed autonomous organization (DAO) allows networked collaboration without hierarchy and intermediaries, and may be the perfect solution for improving science.

Chapter 10

Distributing Science

How does this all come together? We have seen that science is valuable; how research contributes to evidence-based medicine; and how this knowledge is translated into practice. We have also explored how this process is often slow and imperfect, with many opportunities for improvement. We have looked at blockchain, a new tool that may be applied to these problems; what it is; what it isn't; and where it is and can be used. We have covered some of the industries where this technology is advancing most rapidly, and where it is gaining footholds in health and medicine. Now we look at how it all fits together to improve the engine of science in order to make science better and to accelerate the actionable advancement of medical treatment for improved health outcomes and saving lives; in other words, how it can help achieve faster medical miracles.

Because of the differences in data complexity, people and processes in science, you can't simply plug the fintech blockchain applications into all areas of health research and expect success or even compliance. We first need to dissect science, identify the key areas for application of the technology, compile this vision and figure out how we are going to get there.

The first step is to recognize that science has scaled and specialized but has done so while maintaining a system that compartmentalizes most of the work into silos headed by principal investigators (PIs). Despite massive changes in scope of the enterprise and detail of the execution since the 1950s, this siloed PI structure has been deemed necessary for trust. Nowhere is this more evident than in human-focused research, where in the United States and elsewhere this role and its associated responsibility have been codified in related human research protection laws and regulations.

With blockchain as a new tool to facilitate rapidly auditable trust, it may give us the opportunity to de-silo and hence distribute more efficiently this historically micromanaged trust and research execution.

Beyond One Basket

Traditionally, the majority of biomedical research areas and many other branches of science have been conducted in small teams of individuals headed by a PI. This is the person ultimately responsible for each project from a scientific, ethical, regulatory and fiduciary perspective. They have almost always earned a PhD in their field along with subsequent work (i.e., post-doctoral training) to establish their bona fides in both subject matter knowledge as well as mastery of all phases of the scientific process. Along with the overall responsibility, they also get most of the credit, with others working under guidance doing many of the tasks and receiving credit that somewhat corresponds to their roles. Junior faculty, post-docs, senior graduate trainees and senior research assistants may execute and oversee some or all the aspects of the project as assistant investigators. Junior graduate trainees along with research assistants and technical support team members are those who put in the rest of the work. In the end, it is the PI who will pull everything together: ideation, research design, funding proposals, regulatory approvals, study execution and data collection, data analysis, interpretation and dissemination of findings.

The PI role and the academic training system to achieve it are the foundation of the academic research system. Someone with the end-to-end mastery of all phases of science is considered critical as a position of trust at the lead of each project. It is roughly the equivalent of the head of a car-manufacturing company being required to have demonstrated mastery of developing a concept car, design and specifications, manufacture, safety check, maintenance, sales and distribution.

Most businesses do not run like this, at least not anymore. Scaling and diversification of tasks requires that top leadership and even upper management focus more on aligning specialists across the relevant areas in order to achieve the desired output with maximum quality and efficiency. But science is not a system to produce a known quantity, it is a unique system created to deliver new knowledge. The end-stage products are pieces of new knowledge that can be scrutinized by others, but for which there is no immediate quality test available as there would be for a car or a widget.

In this science and its immediate output, peer-reviewed papers are more like works of art than manufactured products. Unlike a painting or a novel, however, scientific papers and their results are not stand-alone items to be appreciated or ignored, they are the building blocks for future exploration in their field and in quantity become the foundation for evidence-based application of medicine or policy. Because of this, science requires a trusted individual, the PI, to sit at the helm of every project and allow their track record to validate the results.

This dynamic of the trusted PI was once largely aligned with the size and mission of the decentralized scientific enterprise. The main driver for going into science was curiosity, with its exacting tedium and often limited funding. Those who were involved were more often collaborators than competitors, with the vastness of the unknown and the unique focus and specialization of each area of exploration requiring shared curiosity to advance. Individual competition did occur, often notable and vicious, but most fields were able to come together with the lead researchers collaborating at all phases to advance the whole.

Science has scaled considerably over the last 75 years, with rapid expansion in the United States since World War II with Vannevar Bush's direct influence of federal funding for science. The rapidly rising cost of healthcare along with societal impacts of an aging population have led to further increases in the funding and attention to biomedical research over the past several decades. With this expansion in research has come an advance in many areas of health, but also some complex secondary effects that appear to be slowing the rate of return on this research investment.

The number of new PhDs in biomedical sciences has outstripped the available positions for them to achieve PI status. Where the majority of those who completed doctoral training used to move into tenure-track research faculty roles and extended careers as PIs, now just 10%–15% can hope to achieve that goal. This overabundance of trained talent has led many otherwise qualified potential PIs into other areas beyond research, while also creating a new system of extended post-doctoral training. These "perma-docs" are often stuck in post-doc or non-tenure track faculty positions for a decade or more. This has resulted in the development of mega-labs across many fields of biomedical research, with sometimes dozens of otherwise qualified potential PIs working as AIs or Co-PIs under the lead lab PI. This results in research that is much more homogenous than would be the case if these perpetual post-docs led their own labs.

These labs and their incremental but low risk advance in research are more effective at getting large grant funding then the newer, smaller labs that do appear. While the smaller labs bring novel perspectives and approaches to health research, the risk involved in funding new approaches is also higher. The funding systems, especially in the federal government, are particularly risk-averse, and so the systems for selecting and awarding new funding have been shifting toward the mega-labs over the past couple of decades. Given that the universities housing these researchers receive nearly 50% overhead administrative funds for those research dollars awarded to their labs big and small, they have been incentivized to maintain the mega-labs at the cost of fewer smaller labs, and hence, less innovation.

Adding to this competitive dilemma, the rapid increase in science funding, and the administrative dollars it brings to the university, has led to expanded programs for training new PhD students even as the space for them in the traditional PI roles has not kept pace. These keep the large labs supplied with highly motivated, highly skilled labor for a ridiculously low cost. Biomedical grad students are usually given tuition reimbursement and below minimum wage stipend for what can usually be expected to be an 80+ hours work week for 5–7 years (often having to apply for and receive their own funding in the latter years). This dynamic along with the general perception, and probably reality, that attaching oneself to these mega-labs makes you more likely to gain success in your career has created a system that is giving us bigger and bigger islands of less and less innovation.

These islands are also competing for funding, which makes the collaboration that used to occur across fields now happen primarily only at the latter phases of research when obtaining funding or publishing incremental findings is no longer in jeopardy by talking to your competitors. The competition for funding and findings, and the fear of being scooped has created isolation in an endeavor that thrives on collaboration, and steadily degraded both the economic impact of our research investment and the innovative impact of some of our most innovative minds.

New Model Science

By breaking the scientific process into its component parts using a mission essential task list (METL) method, science can be approached in a new way. This will allow for an increased engagement of scientists across current silos. The emerging blockchain technology can provide the framework for trust for these scientists engaged via a platform marketplace for gig science, the growing trend of freelance scientific research. This will provide both direct network effects from the blockchain network as it grows, along with indirect network effects from the platform model for pairing scientists with funding and ideas with those scientists with skills, availability and time. In the health sciences, this will lead to better science, cheaper research and faster miracles.

Science is thought of and sometimes even described by its practitioners as more artful or intuitive than it actually is. There are certainly aspects of creativity in developing new ideas and appropriately interpreting the results of an experiment, but much of it is a complex series of very simple processes. Each of these is describable, trackable and measurable (though metrics will differ by discipline). Understanding this is a key aspect in understanding science, the challenges with its current execution, and opportunities to improve it with blockchain and distributed ledgers in general.

Mission Essential Task List

A mission essential task list or METL is a general term for an outline of the basic tasks necessary to complete a specific mission. It is utilized in the U.S. military to focus limited resources and ensure details of critical steps necessary for mission are handed off when there is staffing turnover.

The METL used by the military, especially the U.S. Army, aims to enhance mission execution and success in combat situations when resources may be strained, and timeframe may be short. It is a critical focusing agent in a high-stress and life-threatening situation. It is also useful in a slower paced but complex situation like the bureaucracy in Washington, D.C. How to focus resources and actions when there are competing priorities can be a helpful guide.

In 2014–2015, this METL approach was used by the research leadership at the Defense and Veterans Brain Injury Center, a military and veteran traumatic brain injury research network. This was a helpful framework to implement, as the network includes more than a dozen sites in the United States and Europe and approximately 100 researchers working on 60+ research studies, all in the context of clinical care and education mission priorities. There was resistance from the researchers, as many feel their work and process are too complex and intuitive to be broken down in a project planning style task-by-task way. This simply wasn't true. Despite having a diversified research portfolio with studies ranging from simple one person retrospective data analyses to a 15-year prospective, multi-track, longitudinal study with a staff of 50, we were able to align similar tasks, define them down to sub-task, assign and project workload and staffing requirement, describe areas of hard vs. soft scheduling and control, and associate each part with associated standard operating procedures and required training. All of this was traced back to the specific drivers for each individual research project or task, from researcher generated studies with existing resources to congressional mandates, which allowed for prioritization.

Table 10.1 shows METL for science—breakdown of the key tasks and some example sub-tasks involved in scientific research.

Table 10.1   METL for Science

Phase	Major Tasks	Key Sub-Tasks
Pre-research	Idea formation/ hypothesis	Reading literature, identifying gaps, conference attendance, discussion with colleagues.
	Research design	Background, hypotheses, timeline, methods, equipment, resources, data plan, statistical plan, publication plan, roles and responsibilities.
	Funding	Identify funding source, research plan, background, literature context, significance, innovation, specific aims, budget, team, resources, facilities, assurances.
	Regulatory approval	Pre-meeting with regulators, protocol, privacy plan (humans), compliance with regs.
Research	Collect data	Research plan, assurances, hypotheses (if existing databases); recruit and consent patients (if prospective human study), run the experiment, capture raw data, initial processing, quality control.
	Analysis	Run statistical analyses, test hypotheses, test statistical power, produce results report.
Post-research	Interpretation	Review results in the context of study and existing literature, discuss with colleagues, draw conclusions, validate.
	Communication	Create tables and graphs, write up methods, write up conclusions, present findings, consider feedback, identify target publication, submit manuscript for peer-review, share results and publication.

Major Science Tasks

We have covered these eight major task areas in the previous chapter, here they are again for review.

Pre-research
1. **Idea formation/Hypothesis**—Creating a new idea for testing based on previously captured knowledge in the field, observation and sometimes preliminary data.
2. **Research design**—Creating a research protocol that captures the hypothesis to be tested, key aims, methodology, research plan and data analysis plan.
3. **Funding**—Identifying a funding source, giving background context and an explanation of significance to the research plan and completing key administrative details in the appropriate format.
4. **Regulatory approval**—Getting the required regulatory approval to conduct the experiment from the appropriate institutional review boards.

Research execution
5. **Collect data**—Gather the necessary data from recruited patients or pre-existing data sources, capturing key meta-data elements relating to the experimental data and following up for data at a later time point as appropriate.
6. **Analyze**—Doing statistical analyses based on preset hypotheses to be tested to demonstrate statistical significance of the results and statistical power of the data to support those results not simply being random chance.

Post-research
7. **Interpret results**—Drawing conclusions of the results in the context of what is known in the field and interpreting this new evidence into findings.
8. **Share findings**—Describing what research was done in the context of existing information in the field with sufficient detail to allow for independent replication, presenting these findings to colleagues in small groups and at conferences; incorporating feedback; and writing the study, results, and conclusions up for peer-review and publication.

Key Sub-Tasks

Each of these eight task areas in turn contains a host of sub-tasks, sub-sub-tasks, etc. These can differ depending on a variety of criteria, including the type of research, as well as the field of study, the organization or the funding source. Each basic task is describable as an independent action in the context of the whole with an associated standard operating procedure to be followed, quality checks to be made and associated skills and training necessary or recommended for the executor of that task.

It would be too much to include this all in this book. It often exists in pieces for most organizations, though much of it can often be fragmented, scattered or simply inherently known and not captured. I would recommend the exercise of capturing it, in as much detail and including as much variance as possible. The level of granularity will vary by organization, department and individual lab. But the exercise will be a much more understood process that can be transparently shared internally and externally, aligned with best practices, incorporated into project management processes and used as the basis for training and automation for better and more efficient execution of research.

Here is a second level breakdown of sub-tasks in a few key areas. Please note that there is some overlap and input between task areas (e.g., research design informs funding proposals).

Funding Proposals

Abstract/summary—A brief background of the project; specifics aims, objectives and hypotheses; significance of the research; unique aspects and innovation; methodologic steps and details; expected results and a description of potential impact.

Research plan: overview—A description of what you plan to do; why it is worth doing and the innovative aspects of it; background of what has already been done, the context of this proposal, and what it will add to the field; what has been done to establish the feasibility; the key elements of who, what, when, where and why the research will be done.

Research plan: specific aims—Broad long-term goals; specific hypotheses to be tested; summary of expected outcome; impact to the field.

Research plan: significance—State of existing knowledge in the field with relevant literature citation; rationale of the proposed research; gaps in knowledge in the field the research will fill; impact to the field of knowledge.

Research plan: innovation—Explanation of how the research is novel to the field; the innovative aspects of study design and expected research outcomes; any innovative pilot data that has already been collected.

Research plan: approach—Preliminary studies, experimental design, descriptions of the methods and analyses for each specific aim; discussion of potential difficulties and how these can be mitigated; expected results and alternate approaches if unexpected results are found; a project timetable; strategy to establish feasibility (if in early stages); detailed description of how the data will be collected, analyzed and interpreted.

Budget and justification—Breakdown of key costs including personnel, outside consulting and services, equipment, supplies, travel and other expenses.

Assurances—Written assurances and standard forms that the research will be conducted in accordance with all applicable laws and research and workplace regulations.

Resources and environment—Description of the resources and environment to show that it is both appropriate and suitable for the proposed work.

Team description—Curriculum vitae or detailed biosketch for principal investigator(s), senior researcher, and key staff on the project to demonstrate background and capabilities will allow successful completion and interpretation of proposed research.

Data and Analysis

Define hypothesis—Clearly state and define each question being asked and hypothesis to be tested against the data before the data has been collected and reviewed. This is to establish objective, unbiased testing and avoid data fishing expeditions that can lead to false discovery and erroneous results.

Prioritize variables—Of the identified variables being collected including basic or demographic variables, study variables, and outcome variables, identify which are key or most critical in planned analysis and comparison.

Develop analysis plan—Determination of statistical analysis and comparisons to be done with the data that is to be collected.

Collect and store data—Recruit patients; gather key data; clean, store and tag data for uncomplicated retrieval and clear detail for later analysis.

Analyze data—Perform relevant statistical test as planned; consider and justify any additional tests to be conducted.

Test statistical power—Confirm statistical validity or power of results based on study sample size and other key factors.

Create results report—Produce results report with key details and results of analysis in a format for sharing and review in order to facilitate interpretation.

Presentations and Publications

Prepare tables and figures from analyses—Visual display of the key qualitative or quantitative elements and results for easy review and understanding by those familiar with the field and also a broader audience when possible.

Write up methodology—A detailed description of the methodology used to collect the data including process, patient details, collection methods including tests and equipment, references to demonstrate validity of methods and previous successful use, statistical analyses, and key assumptions and limitations to the data.

Write up results including figures—A clear narrative describing the quantitative results in expanded detail.

Discuss results—A discussion of each aspect of the results, whether it met expectations or differed and why.

Develop conclusion—Develop a comprehensive interpretation and conclusion of the results in the context of existing knowledge; what was found and why is it important, consideration of next steps and future studies.

Give background and introduction—A detailed overview of the state of knowledge in the relevant field with citations to previous literature that serves as the foundation for the current study being described; key aspects of the significance of the new research.

Write summary abstract—An overview of all other parts of the publication condensed as a short, brief, publicly accessible (even when the full paper is behind a paywall), self-contained summary abstract.

Until now, the PI was the trusted glue that held the collection of these parts together and validated the findings. With blockchain applications, we can begin to move to a point where a wider variety of PIs, with rapidly auditable systems in place, can validate a wider variety of findings more rapidly, at a lower cost and with a higher level of quality assurance. Eventually, we may be able to largely disintermediate the PI role, allowing for distributed systems of scientists and/or specialists across all phases to execute all phases of science better, cheaper and faster with the right governance, distributed systems and audit processes in place.

What is a scientist? Whereas once we reserved the term for only those involved in the end-to-end process, we have expanded the term to include many of those involved in only some of the various phases, from grad students to research assistants and technical specialists.

As Karmen Condic-Jurkic puts it, there are a number of issues in science mostly because the system is obsolete, as it was designed in the past century when not many people were "doing science."

"And it was mostly men, and then you had professors, thinkers, involved in different fields. There was this romantic notion of the lone genius going on a long walk and having a breakthrough," Karmen says.

We have also begun to broaden the name further with the more recent focus on citizen science, those citizens who may collect data used for scientific research (e.g., Cornell bird watching program). In health research these contributors are still called subjects or patients, though with the rapid rise in data gathering devices (e.g., FitBit) and massive open online studies (e.g., All of Us—NIH) we may be able to include these contributors as citizen scientists as well. What is there was an expansion in opportunity for individuals with the levels of training and certification necessary for each individual task involved in science to be able to contribute as part of the overall team? Could science be broken into subsequent pieces and distributed across a much broader network of individuals for execution of all phases? Let's look at how this would work.

A critical step in distributing science would be validating the necessary skills, quality and trustworthiness of the individual efforts involved. This already occurs in both the recruitment and initial trust of new lab members under a traditional PI, along with engagement with outside companies and freelancers to execute certain tasks. These are most often specialized data analyses and outside medical writers for both the grant proposal and publication phases.

The trust for these current new and outside parties comes from an informal scrutiny of background, training, and education, along with the validation of first-hand knowledge, references, or confirmed examples of the previous work. The process for this is slow, non-standardized and often somewhat random in when and where it is applied. In the short term, more standardized distributed systems can be layered across existing systems and networks to facilitate this trust building in a more rapid and expanded way.

By assigning individuals verifiable identity, education, skills and achievement in a distributed system that can be updated, shared, accessed and searched in real time, we could speed up the current framework of science collaboration.

It has been said that scientists would rather share a toothbrush than data, but this may change with a better system for trust. Many if not all aspects of science can be distributed among people in other labs, with intellectual property, methodology and data alteration tracking through blockchain and associated hashing as the mechanism of trust, along with a system to validate training and skills of the newfound pool of instant collaborators. Similarly, more traditional freelancers can be added to the pool with this same functionality of individual validation and provenance of data and methodology.

What follows next is a system that can be further expanded into different areas of specialty. Just as individual freelancers are currently involved in projects once appropriate trust for the individual and task is established, a wider pool of individuals may be able to be involved in more specialized tasks once appropriate skills training and verification have aligned with an appropriate standard and systems for tracking and auditing output are more firmly in place. If a few thousand high school students can currently be involved with university level research as summer interns each year, why couldn't a few hundred thousand be involved with university level research as part of externships embedded in their science classes each year?

Full METL to Faster Miracles

One of the first steps required to move toward such a system is to break down which phases, tasks, and sub-tasks of science might lend themselves to being distributed; and of these which ones might be distributed via access to a centralized database compared to a blockchain-based distributed system for the speed and quality peer-to-peer sharing and auditability it can bring. The exploration, sub-task by sub-task of what can be distributed and what is the best technology to do that will itself be of value in expanding opportunities, regardless of whether blockchain is the most viable solution for each. One thing to keep in mind is that as we get into specific sub-tasks, there may be differences across sub-disciplines of science. What works for neurology might not work for oncology.

Another aspect to consider is what phases and sub-tasks can be outsourced, to whom and how. This will be easier to establish as near term and long term. In the near term what parts are viable for outsourcing with immediate application of some existing technologies, blockchain and others? In the long term, what becomes possible to outsource as new skill validation and auditing systems are in place? Considering this allows us to compare possibilities to shift away from current bottlenecks.

A network of distributed science will have biphasic network effect enhancing its value and impact. There will be a direct network effect of bringing blockchain to science. The more people who become involved in networks applying blockchain to administrative, peer-review, data management and data sharing, the greater the impact and value will be. This will come from less costly and more rapid grant review via smart contracts, weighted crowdsourced publication peer review for faster review with less bias, auditable and automated data management, and more rapid data sharing and expanded analysis with tracking of intellectual property contribution.

There will also be an indirect network effect of the platform for gig science that blockchain can help facilitate with its trust framework. As more aspects of research are achieved across the platform, more trained scientists not fully employed in the field, as well as nascent gig science workers, will be available to contribute. As cheaper research costs allow for more to be done, this platform market will grow in indirect network effect.

Some nascent efforts are bringing blockchain technology to different aspects of science. At the foundation of this will be a platform for gig science focused on the deconstructed METL areas primed for outsourcing from the traditional scientific silos. Bringing together funded researchers with ideas and money, and available researchers with skills, interest and time under the framework of blockchain trust framework will provide both direct and indirect network effects to give better science, cheaper research and faster miracles.

We have made great strides with what has become a $1.7 trillion annual worldwide cross-industry scientific research and development effort. But our return on that investment has been dwindling. Thankfully, we have the tools and emerging technology to drastically improve the value of research. Across the health science community, there is opportunity and desire to bring better science, cheaper research and faster miracles to society. This can be done and compounded with the direct and indirect network effects of blockchain technology and a platform for bringing researchers together.

Chapter 11

Better Quality Science

The idea of quality, most importantly that scientific findings can be replicated independently and represent an object assessment of the natural world that can be generalized more broadly, is fundamental to science. Without it, we simply have elaborate stories that look like objective reality but are not a solid foundation on which to base action to interact with the world. In medical science, this fundamental is the basis for trust in the evidence that makes up the evidence-based treatments we apply to keep people well or make people get better when they are sick or injured. At the very least they should improve the situation and "do no harm," as outlined in the Hippocratic oath.

As we have seen, this ideal is not always achieved. The fact that approximately 20% [11-1] of the $150 billion of biomedical research is not reproducible is indicative of poor quality. At best, that poor quality translates into slower advances to improving medicine when the noise makes it harder to identify the signal to act upon. At worst, this poor quality can also lead us down the wrong path to improving health, which can lead to bad medical decision-making. This costs time and money, but more importantly, this costs lives and quality of life for those of us and our loved ones in rapid need of care.

If 20% of your groceries were rotten or past expiration date when they were delivered, you would complain, return them and possibly never shop from the same place again. Yet, 20% of the evidence that underlies the pharmaceuticals, devices and therapy we undergo as part of our health treatment is just as bad. It largely just goes unnoticed. If food or drugs we put into our body were this contaminated, there would be immediate steps to identify the source and implement a recall. With the science that underlies the evidence of our evidence-based medicine, no such system exists. It is left to the trusted scientists and institutions that made the mistakes to slowly clean up the errors over the years and generations. For hundreds of years this has been the way, and despite rapid scaling of the scope of research and the more immediate impact of premature findings spread via multi-media channels, we have erected no safeguards. Blockchain is a tool that may allow for cheaper and more rapid auditing at many stages in the medical science pipeline, improving the quality of outcomes and products considerably.

Improved Auditability

The practice of tracking research data and associated details is largely an ad hoc effort by study, lab or multi-site study based on the minimally viable meta-data details to satisfy regulators and funders while keeping a record for writing up a methodology section in subsequent publications. Huge amounts of captured and capturable meta-data is available but not cost-effective or useful to track and incorporate into analyses, interpretation and dissemination.

Considering the research data as a product in a long supply chain—from raw data to cleaned and analyzed database, to disseminated findings to cumulative evidence for application to practice—may allow for additional insights and applications of blockchain to improve science. By capturing meta-data details at each step, data will be easier to audit and verify, as well as more mergeable with related data sets. This will not only improve how data is collected on the front end but also give more value to the overall effort in each field (Figure 11.1).

As referenced earlier, systematic studies have shown that up to 20% of the $150 billion in biomedical research done in the United States is not reproducible. This figure is much higher in some sub-disciplines, with certain areas of experimental psychology estimated to be around 75% being NOT reproducible. These are disturbing numbers. Not only is this research wasted money and effort, but it is also bad information or noise that is fed into the overall record of science. This causes additional studies to be based—and funded—on faulty premises, areas of exploration to be skipped, research funding priorities to be changed and actionable practice or policy to be delayed or based on bad science. The overall cost to society of this kind of bad science is hard to estimate.

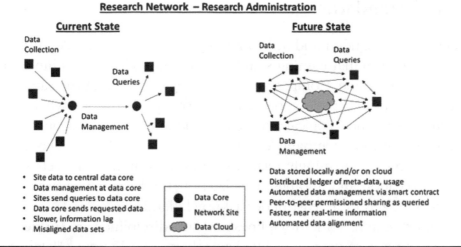

Figure 11.1 Better quality science: how rapid access auditing of scientific data can be enabled with blockchain.

Many factors contribute to this reproducibility crisis. Most of this lack of reproducibility is not due to overt fraud (less than 0.05% of scientific papers are retracted [11-2]) but instead is often the result of rushed or sloppy science. Studies [11-3] have shown that even intermittent, random auditing of data and analyses can cut the problems with them nearly in half. The audits serve as a double check and reinforcement of best practices which incentivizes taking the time to get the science right. This level of auditing, particularly by a third party is not currently viable from a time, cost and permissions aspect. With the introduction of a blockchain/DLT system and associated hashing of data sets, new layers of quality control can be added, with inexpensive and rapid auditing now more viable. This could lead to billions of dollars in savings each year, as well as accelerating the overall movement from research to practice by reducing the noise and speeding up the process of accumulating necessary levels of evidence to affect practice.

This advanced tracking and improved auditability of research data will have a major impact on cleaning up science and give a better signal-to-noise ratio in what comes from our research efforts. This higher quality science will not only have an immediate impact on reducing problems with reproducibility and giving us more actionable findings, it will also clean up the overall quality of research findings. Every new finding is the foundation for future findings, and the reliability of this body of evidence keeps scientists motivated to continue building on these foundations.

Improved Standards

As science has expanded and scaled rapidly over the last half century, little effort has gone into maintaining standards in data collection within each field and sub-discipline. Competing methodologies aimed at the same problem are important to a wide approach to problem-solving, but when scaled too far without methodological and data element alignment produces results and findings that look comparable but are not. The result has been the inability to compare seemingly related studies or combine data sets for more detailed exploration and findings. This lack of standards is pervasive and often unrecognized or at least under acknowledged.

In health research, some disciplines and sub-disciplines are further along in creating core data elements than others. The National Database for Autism Registry (NDAR) was one of the first major efforts in brain research to address this lack of data standards and create standard autism research elements that would allow for the aggregation of data across studies into a single database for cross-study comparison and meta-analyses [11-4]. This shared database created the opportunity to get more impact from research investment.

Modeled after the NDAR, the Federal Interagency Traumatic Brain Injury Research (FITBIR) informatics system was developed by the DoD, National Institutes of Health (NIH) and U.S. Department of Veterans Affairs as a shared research database utilizing standard common data elements developed in the 2000s by a group of academic and government TBI research experts. This centralized database came online in the early 2010s and is now housed at the NIH. Other research areas such as specific types of cancer have also achieved some level of shared standards to facilitate more research. Other areas such as mental and psychological health are still working with smaller pockets of aligned standards, but lack more universally accepted and utilized standard data elements.

There are tremendous benefits to standards including validation of reproducibility across studies and merging data sets for addition analysis and greater statistical power. Additionally, it allows for making the combined data sets available to additional researchers for more analysis to answer a greater number of questions and perform meta-analyses. This all can contribute to moving from research to actionable findings in a shorter amount of time, at a lower cost and with greater reliability.

Blockchain can become a forcing function to achieving these standards in each area. The efforts to create standards require significant cost and collaboration. Only in limited cases (e.g., Autism and TBI) has there been a sufficient push by funding agencies and advocates to make it happen. Blockchain can create a new value proposition to the effort to create standards. With more value achievable for each discipline and sub-discipline of health research, it becomes worth the short-term cost (i.e., experts' time to develop consensus along with facilitation costs) for the greater long-term benefit blockchain can bring to each effort.

Cross-discipline approaches to develop these standards have already begun. There are multiple layers of standards to consider, from the overarching technical standards to the semantic and syntactic data that become unique to each area of research. These will need to align with existing standards both technical (i.e., FIHR/HL7) or data element related (i.e., NDAR, FITBIR). Initially the process of determining where existing standards suffice, harmonizing with other ongoing efforts, and identifying those areas of research that may need to be divided or bundled to achieve common data elements sufficient to facilitate combined research data sets will be required. NIST, Institute of Electrical and Electronics Engineers (IEEE) Standards Association, International Organization for Standards (ISO), FIHR and others have begun some work on technical standards that can be applied to or are specific to blockchain in healthcare.

For research and looking to specific data standards across disciplines, some areas have developed standards that can be borrowed, but many others will need to develop consensus in order to take advantage of this technology. The IEEE Standards Association group devoted to blockchain in healthcare and health, life and social sciences has a research sub-group that is identifying what can be borrowed from and what needs to be created to implement this technology across the more than 200 sub-disciplines of health and life sciences research.

Meta-Analysis Capabilities

If you recall from the Levels of Evidence Pyramid from Chapter 7, Figure 7.2, meta-analyses are at the top. These analyses are conducted across multiple studies, sometimes looking at the same question and sometimes looking at new questions across similar data. The value in these studies is that they are both using a larger body of data which generally provides more statistical significance and statistical power to the findings. It also combines data from multiple sources, which minimizes the impact of bias, error or bad methodology in any given study. Ideally, the data that is merged should measure the same thing in each and have been collected in similar ways. Unfortunately, this is not always the case. It can still be valuable to run the meta-analyses with some slight variance in the way it was collected, but this will lead to more noise and less signal in the results.

Chapter 12

Value-Based Research

The value of scientific research is universally accepted and yet very difficult to measure on a broad scale. In health research, individual companies can track their ROI in localized scale, yet the same measure of return for government funded and academic research is limited. Most research ROI for publicly funded research is focused on the immediate economic impact: how many jobs does it create and how does it boost the economy. The more long-term return in the form of improved care, healthcare cost savings, lives saved and improved quality of life is much more elusive. This is partly due to the difficulty of attribution across multiple cycles of research, as well as to the extended timeline, years to decades, before real clinical impact.

Blockchain stands to transform this value equation in several ways. A combination of monetary fractionalization, micro-tracking and longitudinal records has already been developed with cryptocurrency charity tracking, for example. Mirroring this approach, research funding organizations should be able to track research dollars more acutely, as well as the fractional involvement each study may have on subsequent research along with the impact of eventual treatments put into practice.

This will transform comparative effectiveness research into a new level of granular assessment of the value of research we'll call value-based research. Second, the use of smart contracts with blockchain application to data management and analysis will allow for significant automation and cost savings.

Third, the basic administrative blockchain applications that have already begun transforming and streamlining administrative processes in the federal government and elsewhere can be applied to a variety of administrative aspects of research. This will speed up the process, reduce costs and

Figure 12.1   Value-based research: the ability to track research dollars and their fractional impact more granularly will provide a system demonstrate the value of every research dollar spent. Traditionally, research ROI assessment has been difficult because of extended time lag (average of 17 years) and difficulty to assigning weighted attribution for individually funded studies contributing to eventual improved health outcomes and related savings.

accelerate findings. In other words, this will improve outcomes and save lives (Figure 12.1).

Increased ROI

Vannevar Bush's "Science the Endless Frontier" in the 1950s captured the value of U.S. federally funded research and development during World War II and successfully argued for that impact to be integrated into a peacetime effort to spur the economy and advance the science and engineering advancements to transform the country. As outlined in Chapter 8, this resulted in the founding of the National Science Foundation and eventually to what would become the National Institutes of Health (NIH).

This latter half of the 20th century saw a continual rise in federal funding for basic and applied research. This was done in conjunction with related industries who created a steady stream of new products through advanced development based on these findings.

In health research, major pushes in cancer, cardiology and brain research became the drivers for an ever-expanding marketplace of new treatments, better health and extended longevity through these decades. This U.S. advancement was mirrored in Europe and parts of Asia initially, and eventually became a worldwide area of government funded research. Specific health interest and funding agencies in the form of non-profit foundations and professional societies followed and refined this model.

This research funding has been shown to be a major economic driver through the direct impact on economies from creation of jobs and new products [12-1]. What has been widely accepted but more difficult to quantify is that this same effort has positive and quantifiable impact on the field in which the research occurred. Health research contributed to better health and longer life as a whole, but it was more difficult to measure the impact of any particular study. In turn, this made the funding decisions across the extended bench to bedside cycle more reliant on the state-of-the-art knowledge of experts rather than anything scientific.

In recent decades however, there has been a growing effort to begin to track the direct impact of health research [12-2]. This process has been difficult for several reasons [12-3], including the extended time to impact; the diffuse worldwide nature of science and the difficulty in tracking attribution across the multiple cycles of research that integrate to become actionable knowledge. The systems as they currently stand are not set up to make this type of economic impact tracking easy. The most promising approaches are siloed or ad hoc. This has hamstrung efforts to make funding decision-making and resource prioritization to health problem-solving more targeted and successful. The recent U.S.-based "cancer moonshot" is more of a money dump on existing cancer research with some general nods toward innovation. With the effort to get to the moon in the 1960s, the target was known and hence funding was focused on engineering innovation with the best available scientific knowledge to get there. On the contrary, with the cancer moonshot, we don't know where the moon is or the best way to get there. We need to first find the "moon" in incremental steps, but we also have no system for feedback to learn from previous efforts beyond the analog and potentially biased system of expert opinion. From an administrative evidence standpoint, we are at the bottom of the levels of evidence pyramid (i.e., expert opinion) in trying to determine what will work.

Value-based health research is the idea that we can better track the value and impact of individual research throughout the bench to bedside lifecycle to provide more refined feedback on research gaps, funding, methodology and successful approaches. The tracking will steadily improve our ROI for research, save money toward more and better research and allow more rapidly reaching actionable findings that have a positive impact on patient outcomes. While it's true that this is all doable with current technology, it's prohibitively complicated and exorbitantly expensive to make it viable and sustainable blockchain adds a new layer to this process by being a new tool to make tracking diffuse and fractionalized attribution of research dollars to impact more achievable.

Reduced Data Management Costs

Smart contracts are automated processes that can be coded into a blockchain protocol based on shared governance rules on how certain types of data are to be managed and processed. This aspect of blockchain application will add a new layer of speed, cost savings and quality to not only administrative processing facilitated by blockchain but also specific application to research data management and basic analysis. This will be faster, cheaper and more reliable than current manual data cleaning, quality assurance and quality control.

In current health research, much of the data management is still performed manually. This is often extremely time consuming and expensive, especially in smaller labs where the senior researchers must split time from more specialized tasks with the mundane and repetitive management. It is also a source of considerable quality control challenges, with manual manipulation of large amounts of data resulting in human error being introduced to the system.

Blockchain application with smart contracts can be used for data management and first-line data analysis. This standardized and automated data cleaning and processing can save tremendous time and cost, while providing a more reliable, higher quality data set. The rapidly and transparently auditable nature of blockchain also allows for auditing by the researchers, collaborators, administrators and even peer-reviewers in a way that was conceivable with existing technology but ultimately cost prohibitive.

Data monitoring for clinical trials is another area where application of this technology can have significant impact. Phase 1 trials, which help determine effective drug dosage, and phase 2 trials, which establish drug efficacy for the condition in question, especially require ongoing monitoring to ensure data quality and patient safety. If you are giving a test drug to a large number of patients to test safety and validity, you want to be able to know quickly—and in quasi real-time—if there are any major concerns, and it is critical at the time of analysis to have verifiably clean data as it is aggregated from multiple sources.

There is global concern that this type of automation may reduce jobs. But this prospect seems unlikely in the case of science. Of course, in some instances, there may need to be retraining or refocusing, but this will largely be done within the same system and skill set. Initial impact will likely be to automate aspects of the administration, execution and publishing [12-4] of scientific research.

This will represent more of an opportunity for those involved to focus on other tasks: the administrators can more rapidly facilitate new research and refine the process for decision-making on the best research investments and scientists and related technical experts can do more science. For every question asked in science, two or more new ones arise. The automation that blockchain can facilitate will expand the field rather than contract it.

Chapter 13

Faster Medical Miracles

Speed saves. It saves lives and it saves money, which in turn can save more lives, when it comes to medical research. We've seen that it takes 17 years to get new treatment ideas vetted through research and into general treatment of patients. We've also established that this time is made up of numerous time-consuming steps, some being more efficient than others. By applying blockchain in different manners to these steps, life-saving speed can be brought to the research process, along with cost-saving effectiveness and an overall increase in the quality of the research evidence produced for the evidence-based medicine. These applications for the research process range from administrative to data management, with advanced combinations allowing for more rapid and widespread data sharing than has ever before been feasible in the scientific community.

Regulatory and Administration

The human research protection (HRP) regulations that govern clinical research are crucial for protecting patients and their privacy. The critical step of receiving regulatory approval for each new clinical trial is a time-consuming process governed by an institutional review board (IRB) convened at each research facility where they meet only periodically (e.g., once a month). This creates a paperwork-heavy and detail-heavy process involving several parties, repeated verification of key documents and signoffs, and frequent auditing both randomly and for cause to ensure all standards are being met. The result of all this redundancy is a lot of time and personnel resources that go into IRB approvals, amendments and HRP audits.

The complexity and time involved are even exponentially more significant when dealing with multi-site studies crossing organizational lines. The nature of IRBs found at each site is that they are made up of local experts and community representatives with sometimes differing interpretation of what meets the standard of acceptable research. Getting consensus between these groups can take several iterations of IRB interaction at disjointed intervals. Because of this discombobulated process, the bottom line is that IRB approval can take months and in some cases years. This approval is required for any research study to begin, so the delays make each stage of research take longer before it can begin.

Some federal funding agencies in the United States have begun requiring lead IRB for multi-site studies to minimize this burden and try to streamline the process, and many organizations have begun adopting electronic document systems to expedite regulatory approval. This has helped, sure, but many inefficiencies remain. Application of a distributed ledger of which regulatory documents and their data elements have been submitted, approved, amended, expired and renewed could create an efficient system for front end application by the researchers that would save them time and money. It would have the additional value of creating approval and auditing efficiencies for the regulators that would provide their own time and cost savings while also providing more protections for patient safety and data privacy through this cheap and rapid auditing.

The review process for grant applications to determine the research to be funded is another administrative area with considerable delay and redundancy. The time it takes for grant proposal review is usually months, and for larger grants such as the National Institutes of Health (NIH) R01 series, usually 12 months or longer. Adding to this, researchers often need to apply multiple times before successfully receiving a grant, frequently repeatedly entering the same information to the same system of the same funding source. This process takes valuable time away from some of our best and brightest researchers trying to resolve our most pressing health issues. The time it takes for internal administrative processes that include technical review of the proposal by experts further extends the time the whole process takes.

As Arrieta at the U.S. Department of Health & Human Services puts it, "cancer researchers should not spend their time learning processes and regulations. They should spend their time researching cancer."

While key aspects of the grant proposal review process like the expert reviews themselves require sufficient time to be completed, much of the process can be streamlined.

Successful blockchain pilots, such as the one at Government Services Administration (GSA), have reduced the overall time it takes for vendor proposal review by a staggering 90% (110 days to under 10 days) with a similar reduction in cost [13-1]. There are some differences in the level of involvement of required expert technical review for grants, but many of the same components of the process and redundancies are similar enough to follow the GSA template.

Reduction in the repeated entry of information facilitated by the information provenance tracking and verification blockchain can bring along with the automated speed of smart contract application could speed the process, reduce burden on the researchers and get research funds out faster for faster discovery.

In a similar fashion, scientific conferences and publishing contain an array of administrative processes that could be sped with similar application of blockchain in different manners. Anywhere information is redundantly required to simply re-verify its authenticity each time across multiple parties could be a target for blockchain's ability to provide this record of validated trust to reduce time and cost. It can also speed up permissioned accessing of that information whether it is the researchers, reviewers, editors, administrators or intended audience that needs to see and verify the information involved.

Data Management

The management of research data is a complex part of the research process. It is costly and time consuming. It is also the source of a significant part of the reproducibility issues plaguing science. Maintaining data integrity while collecting, combining, cleaning, standardizing, analyzing and sharing the data and data sets involved, has a lot of room for unintentional error that can impact the value of the data as well as impact the findings that relate to it. Many different solutions are used to try and minimize these errors at the cost of considerable time, resources and limits to the access of data. Even with this, it is often not possible to identify and track back errors.

The way data management is approached varies across fields, organizations and even sometimes within individual labs. So, because of this heterogeneous approach, any type of fix or improvement is very limited in their impact. It's true that for larger research networks and consortia, some level of standardization exists, but this happens often at the cost of having a centralized data repository at one of the sites. In turn, this can create new types of risk for the consolidated data, while still not necessarily solving the problem of being able to identify, track back and isolate problematic data.

The solutions blockchain could bring to research data management are still being explored. It seems like some of the advances in using the technology for supply chain management (e.g., food safety, pharma) could be similarly applied to data management when looking at research as a supply chain of data that extends over years and decades. The raw material (data) is gathered and stored. It undergoes initial prep (standardization) and advanced processing (analysis). Advanced products (findings) are further processed and shipped to suppliers and end users (publications).

Exploration of potential distributed solutions for research data management have begun on a small scale across university labs and the pharma industry. Applications at the research network level are also being explored and may offer the most impactful use case because of the multiple parties involved across different systems. Unlike other new technological fixes for this area, blockchain solutions in many cases are compatible with whatever the existing legacy system is and will allow for it to be a value-added addition rather than a costly replacement.

Intellectual Property and Data Sharing

The reason that scientists do not like sharing their pre-funding ideas and their data is that they don't want to be scooped. Scooped refers to someone taking a scientist's ideas or data and getting funding or published results for them faster. Whether it is a lab that has more resources to move things forward faster, or researchers with more insightful perspectives on interpreting data. The most famous case of a scientist getting scooped is that of Rosalind Franklin and Nobel Prize winners Watson and Crick [13-2].

All were among several labs working to identify the structure of DNA. Franklin and her lab had superior X-ray crystallography equipment and techniques. They had submitted a paper with a recent image of DNA and their interpretation as to the structure, which happened to be incorrect. A reviewer of the paper, assessing that the interpreted shape was wrong, showed the picture to colleagues including Watson and Crick. They assessed the double helix structure and published on this finding that they may have never reached on their own. Watson and Crick won the Nobel Prize, Franklin got scooped.

Blockchain provides the structure for capturing the contribution and intellectual property details of research data in a trackable and virtually immutable way. This may provide the trusted structure needed to allow for more open and early data sharing among scientists, while preserving the contribution of the individuals. Some of this is a technological fix, but some of this will require a change in culture.

The tracking of individual contribution of scientists to their research can be greatly enhanced by the application of blockchain. With this detail captured as a meta-data element for each datum, database, statistical test, hypothesis, finding, interpretation and presented or published result, who did what can be preserved and proven even as new data sharing comes into play. It will also be possible to track micro-contributions across research teams in much more granular fashion than is currently possible. With this contribution tracking in place, scientists will become more comfortable sharing data. Once this is established as the safe new norm, more value can be achieved from the same data in a shorter time.

Standards and Meta-Analysis

Another way blockchain may bring enormous benefit to the health research industry is through its potential value making to achieve data standardization across specific fields and areas of research. Many fields of medical research struggle from lack of data standards. This renders cross-study comparisons and replications difficult and impedes the progress toward impactful findings and improved outcomes. While it is generally considered a good idea—in theory—to develop data standards for a particular area of research, many other areas either have competing standards or no real standards at all. It is difficult and time consuming to develop widely accepted standards. The traumatic brain injury common data element standards developed by the DoD, NIH and U.S. Department of Veterans Affairs along with academic and industry experts and used for the Federal Interagency Traumatic Brain Injury Research (FITBIR) informatics system took nearly a decade to develop at considerable cost for regular coordination and facilitation between the participants. If there is no driving participant to foot the bill as the federal government did in this case, data standardization doesn't happen or is only partial or piecemeal.

What blockchain changes is not the ability to create the standards (thought there may be some administrative applications that can help and cost savings with other application to make it more feasible), but a change in the value proposition of what can be done if those standards are in place. With standardized data, and a secure, transparent and rapid system of tracking data, secondary variable, research access and researcher contribution, there will be more use and value extracted from the data. This makes achieving the standards a more valuable goal to pursue and underwrite because of the value it brings to blockchain facilitated research.

In addition, the merging of data sets can provide tremendous levels of analytical insight based on increased statistical power, if the data can be appropriately merged. Data standardization is at the heart of whether or not merging brings value or noise to the combined data set. Understanding and verifying the methodological sourcing of the data is another component that contributes to the value of the merged data. Data collected in similar ways, representing the same type of measurement can safely be merged, whereas data combined across differentiated methodology or secondary variables (e.g., type of machine used to collect data) can be a hidden reason to not merge data. Blockchain offers new levels of assurance in gathering and tracking this methodological detail of each data point, allowing other researchers to be confident in the value of a whole data set independent of trust and verification with each individual contributor.

Blockchain can also be used to facilitate more rapid access to these merged data sets. In existing centralized merged data sets, there is a significant amount of effort that goes into controlling and maintain access to the data. Gatekeepers need to confirm a variety of factors of those they grant access to in order to assure both scientific integrity and regulatory appropriateness of the use. A blockchain system could allow for smart contract controlled automated access for those with the appropriate credentials and regulatory approval. It could also allow for longitudinal record of who accessed the data, when, with what approval/authority, which hypotheses it was tested against, with what statistical methodology and the resulting findings.

This type of system for cloud or central server-based data would allow for faster, safer, controlled access (it can take months to get access to current shared data like that in FITBIR) without the costly intermediary. It would also allow for a record of all who had accessed it, what questions they asked and what they found. This would provide a more complete record of research on the data and avoid unwanted redundancy or effort.

On the other hand, sometimes you need to have redundancy in scientific inquiry in order to confirm findings and authenticate reproducibility.

As review and audit of data becomes easier, a confirmation step as built in quality assurance can become the standard. As data is merged into a shared data set, findings based on the initial data could be confirmed against the whole. This could be completed by those outside the research group for greater validity. It would add to the improvement of the reproducibility issues.

The overall benefit these types of applications of blockchain to health research could generate would be to bring more researchers to the table to create more findings, more verification, at less cost and at an improved speed. More quality findings would advance the state of the science ahead faster in every field of research and bring health improving and lifesaving advances to the public faster than ever before. Faster Miracles.

Chapter 14

DAO of Science

How do we get to the point of accelerated findings and improved health outcomes? How do we use these rapidly developing technological tools to improve the quality, cost and pace of medical research? How do we pave the way for a full scale, mainstream adoption?

The answer is that we first need an accurate picture of the current state of the major moving parts in the system of medical research, and then we need to identify those areas in need of improvement. This includes real-world behavior and incentive models of key stakeholders at all levels of the health research ecosystem: researchers, patients, providers, administrators, funders and publishers. Then, we need a vision of the future incorporating many of the possibilities outlined in the earlier chapters. Finally, we need a realistic plan to get there. It is not enough to have a grand plan to over-haul medical research with new tech tools in one fantastical leap that has no connection with reality and no realistic way to incentivize stakeholders to agree. Instead, we need a practical plan with interim steps and cascading behavioral incentives across all stakeholders.

ConsenSys Health's Flannery devised a framework to that end—the Population Health Impact (PHI) framework, which includes three stages and is a way to think about how to move forward. In essence, she tells us, use cases that have traction currently have a common feature in that they don't use PHI: they either work with public data, such as providers directory data, or work with back office data, such as drug supply chain. That's stage 1.

Stage 3, she says is "our nirvana kind of use cases." She explains that it involves PHI, confirmed identity and being able to orchestrate clinical and scientific processes across organizational boundaries, such as precision medicine and the web3 advanced digital therapeutics that not only lowers costs but really changes outcomes for patients and accelerates innovations to get to faster miracles.

"We can't just stay in stage 1 forever and we can't just move to nothing into full scale mainstream adoption. So, the way to do it, is through research-oriented path, it's right for our industry, for our values and we can do it now. We don't need to wait. The technology is ready."

One of the key aspects to be determined in such a plan is where the decision-making sits, particularly with respect to publicly funded science. Currently, the main decision points of what is funded and what is published/disseminated sits with the main funding organizations (e.g., government and non-profit) and with publishers, respectively. These decisions are informed by the input of the community of experts, facilitated and ultimately controlled by these intermediaries. It is here that blockchain can play a major role. The technology will enable direct peer-to-peer governance of these processes, with rapid controlled access to just-in-time information, automated processing of information to facilitate decision-making. In addition, it will create a shared ledger of input for contribution tracking, and rapid, crowdsourced auditing as a constant check & balance.

With the framework of Open Science and the secure and automated advances of blockchain and other emerging tech, it is now possible to bring science as it stands at its current scale back to its peer-to-peer roots with no major intermediary involvement. This type of blockchain-based distributed autonomous organization (DAO) is being explored across different industries with some small successes and notable failures. Here we make the case that this structure is ideal for much of the medical science enterprise, but like a thousand-foot cliff it needs to be climbed through secure interim steps, rather than all in one step. With this DAO structure in place and advanced technical tools like robotic automated processes, machine learning (ML) and eventually artificial intelligence (AI) applied, scientific and medical advancement will save and improve lives on a scale like we have barely imagined.

ConsenSys Health's Flannery says that in her view, the single most strategic application of blockchain in healthcare is to control and govern the administration of decentralized ML algorithms.

"This will give us the opportunities to make discoveries and will accelerate the pace at which we're learning in a way that is unprecedented in human history," Heather tells us.

This convergence of emerging technologies for what is called "federated learning" will be crucial. This will allow blockchain access control and tracking for ML algorithms to access sensitive (i.e., personal health information) in a secure and limited fashion.

Pulling It All Together

Open Science provides the blueprint for how to envision what science can achieve when functioning at maximum capacity. It has been mostly conceptual or limited in its overall application over the past couple decades. There are a variety of reasons for this, and active and passive forces that may be inhibiting movement toward what the Open Science efforts can achieve.

Blockchain changes the value proposition for tackling many of the widespread collaborative efforts needed to bring this Open Science blueprint to life for widespread adoption. It may serve as the framework, structure and scaffolding in different aspects of each phase and discipline of science.

Robotic processing automation (RPA), ML and AI will allow for the augmentation speed and quality necessary to assist researchers and administrators in all phases of research to handle large volumes of data and fully realize much of the blockchain-facilitated value of Open Science. Outsourcing and gig work in connection with related distributed structures of trust will allow for many more complex portions in different phases of science to be executed more rapidly and less expensively by a wider range of participants, opening up almost endless possibilities. All of this with improved quality and to the benefit of all involved.

The introduction of blockchain/DLT to science will deliver better science, cheaper research and faster miracles. Scientific research is the systematic investigation of the world around us. This process has provided the foundational knowledge upon which discovery and advancement in medicine has made strides forward; the human-driven miracles that save lives.

Science has a critical function in our society, but its complexity and scale have outgrown the institutional structure and standard execution of the process. This has resulted in less than fully utilized resources, slowing of advancement compared to investment and an incentive system that often rewards the trappings of discovery rather than the value of discovery itself.

As discussed in Chapter 10, the military has an effective way of dissecting complex missions and prioritizing tasks and resources in the form of a mission essential task list (METL). Applying this METL template to scientific research could help break the process down into essential tasks, sub-tasks, sub-sub-tasks, etc. These tasks can then be evaluated for complexity of execution with many of them being able to be automated or executed outside the traditional laboratory/clinic silos. This outsourcing of specialized tasks, or gig work, has become commonplace in many industries, but has gained limited traction in the close-held world of science.

There is currently no widely used gig platform for health science. There are freelance medical writers, some limited science forums and a smattering of health science research opportunities on larger sites like Upwork, but gig work has not become common in the health sciences. This is despite 50% overhead costs on research grant money at most universities, significant delays in full-time hiring and a hugely underemployed highly skilled population of scientists outside of the traditional academic setting.

The main challenges to a widely used platform for gig science are (1) difficulty in separating out simple, outsourceable tasks from what has traditionally been an idea-to-publication role for principal investigators and small, contained teams and (2) a lack of trust in sharing certain parts of the process based on concerns of "getting scooped" or losing intellectual property control.

METL for research allows us to dissect the sub-tasks that can be automated or outsourced. But we still need a framework for trust. Blockchain/DLT is maturing at the right time to be the trust framework for gig science and much more. This will create a network of distributed science for better science, cheaper research and faster miracles.

A network of distributed science will have biphasic network effect enhancing its value and impact. There will be a direct network effect of bringing blockchain to science. The more people who become involved in networks applying blockchain to administrative, peer-review, data management and data sharing, the greater the impact and value will be. This will come from less costly and more rapid grant review via smart contracts, weighted crowdsourced publication peer-review for faster review with less bias, auditable and automated data management, and more rapid data sharing and expanded analysis with tracking of intellectual property contribution.

Beyond this, there will be an indirect network effect of the platform for gig science that blockchain can help facilitate with its trust framework. As more aspects of research are achieved across the platform, more trained scientists not fully employed in the field, as well as nascent gig science workers, will be available to contribute. As cheaper research costs allow for more to be done, this platform market will grow in indirect network effect.

The current environment of health science research requires 17 years to go from "bench to bedside," or idea to cure. While some of this time is critical for the appropriate testing and experimentation, significant portions are artifacts of an antiquated system. Reducing the time in grant and publication review as well as regulatory approval could shorten this time by 2–5 years. Reduced costs can afford more research to occur in parallel, allowing for an expanded network effect of shared data. Expanded gig science opportunities will grow the available two-sided platform market of funded researchers with developed hypotheses to test along with available gig researchers with skills to contribute.

Currently there is a lack of infrastructure to support either a platform for science or the application of blockchain. The challenge is to develop these innovations in parallel to help bolster the implementation of each. The widespread use of a platform for gig science will gain more traction with the trust of blockchain. And the value proposition of blockchain for health sciences research will be optimized with the existence of more expanded use across a broad distributed network.

There are some nascent efforts to bring this blockchain technology to different aspects of science by various startups and established pillars in the scientific publishing industry. At the foundation of this will be a platform for gig science focused on the deconstructed METL areas primed for outsourcing from the traditional scientific silos. Bringing together funded researchers with ideas and money, and available researchers with skills, interest and time under the framework of blockchain and trust will provide both direct and indirect network effects to give better science, cheaper research and faster miracles.

The effort to create a network for distributed science is in a very early stage. There are a few challenges to the creation and implementation of this effort. First, there is the culture of science, which has longstanding investment in its current structure and function. It will take a proper tracking of the current system and its multi-layered incentive system to plan the proper strategy for success. On the other side, the complexity of the science incentive system may delay the adoption of blockchain technology in some areas of science where questions, mission and non-monetary incentive structure are more powerful drivers than money. The key will be to map the motives, incentives and goals of the broader scientific community and ensure that the introduction of this new technology is in line with these values.

Science is one of the most valuable efforts of humanity. We have made great strides with what has become a $1.7 trillion annual cross-industry research and development effort. But our return on that investment has been dwindling. Thankfully, we have the tools and emerging technology to drastically improve the value of research. Across the health science community, there is opportunity and desire to bring better science, cheaper research and faster miracles to society. This can be done and compounded with the direct and indirect network effects of blockchain technology and a platform for bringing researchers together.

There are many individual and organizational stakeholders involved in health research, and it will be critical to have all of these involved in designing this expanded future. At the same time, the questions of who will take the lead in any coordination of effort and who will oversee this whole system once it is operational are critical. Who currently runs science and who should run this advanced system? (Figure 14.1)

Science is a distributed system without a clear overall hierarchy. Each field and sub-discipline differs, but overall the leading researchers in each area tend to populate key positions in research, professional societies and editorial boards of related peer-reviewed publications. These bodies serve as the closest thing to a system of controls with respect to the products and outputs of science, with the publishing companies playing a significant role as well. On the front end, funding agencies, public and private, set the research priorities and deliver the necessary funds, often with screening systems made up of many of the same researchers in the output part of the system. In between are the researchers themselves, spread across various academic, government, and private organizations, each with their own administrative

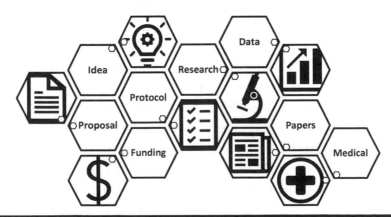

Figure 14.1 Current model of health research: an overview of the key stakeholders and interactions in health research.

systems in play. There is a layer of regulatory controls at all levels, and a feedback system from the scientific output back into the funding organizations that set the research priorities. Output moves into policy and practice in coordination with these same and related organizations (e.g., hospitals and medical professional organizations and societies), often with additional layers of peer-based refining of information and guidelines.

It could be argued that researchers run research, via peer-to-peer systems embedded at each layer, with structural support from funding, administrative and publishing organization that have grown up around the need for trusted intermediaries. These have developed over decades and centuries in an organic, analog fashion. Some efforts have been made to align them and introduce assistive technologies, but these have not been comprehensive or attempted to be transformational in any respect (Figure 14.2).

It could also be argued that the shared governance of the researchers themselves runs research, with the associated organizational overhead as tax for continuous operations at scale.

What is now, or will soon be, possible with blockchain and associated emerging technology could be transformational, but to fully realize the value, some of the structures we know around science may have to be reconsidered.

Distributed Autonomous Science

Distributed autonomous organization (DAO) is a relatively recently developed term for an organization that runs without leadership or hierarchical structure, based on a shared system of governance utilizing a blockchain to execute the

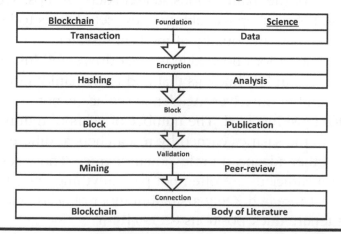

Figure 14.2   Science as analog blockchain: science conceptualized as an analog blockchain with key points of trust identified.

rules of governance automatically via smart contract. This is a new conceptualization made possible by the technologies on which it is meant to be operated. There have been several attempts to create an operational DAO at scale with some limited success and one catastrophic failure [14-1].

Science, as a system, operates in some ways like a precursor to a DAO, or an interlocking series of them across phases and fields. The governance of science is already established in many ways required to set up DAO. Indeed, there have been attempts to describe how the current structure could be layered into a DAO system [14-2]. The challenge is that it is not a one-size-fits-all effort, and different phases and fields may require differing standards of governance. Science is a complex series of systems and would require a complex DAO or a complex series of more simplistic DAOs in theory.

In practice, while these DAO precursor governance structures may be in place, and the more detailed governance needed by phase and field possible, there is no incentive to the average researcher to move to such a structure. And for the current organizations involved in intermediating the governance of science: funders, administrators and publishers; there is a distinct disincentive to help this along in the short term.

Incentives

Trying to get the incentives right in science is not simply a matter of looking at the monetary incentives. There are also different types of non-monetary incentives for those contributing to science, and different types of over-arching incentives for the main various stakeholders' groups. We need to understand these before simply creating a new set of tools to be applied to improve the speed, cost and quality of medical research.

In general, the quest for knowledge is what drives and inspires researchers—a quest and its findings that add to humanity's understanding of the world and of ourselves. Academic science is not a widely lucrative endeavor for most involved. The number of years of training and hours work compared to the salaries earned by researchers at different levels are not on par with other advanced professional degrees. Those researchers who are also well-paid clinicians are often not paid anything extra for the work they do to conduct research. Only a small number of academic biomedical researchers get tenure track positions (<15%) [14-3].

It is that quest that motivates the researchers; the graduate students making less than minimum wage for years; the post-doctoral candidates who work longer hours and make less money than they could in retail management; the adjunct and junior faculty with only a modest chance of a comfortable tenure track position who can work 80+ hours a week for years.

The desire for good science and for getting the findings right accounts for some motivation. Career advancement and taking the steps to advance in a scientific career even if chances at a tenured position are often fleeting, but the excitement of discovery and having rare or unique knowledge of the world, coupled with the contribution to the advancement of knowledge, and getting credit for said contributions are some of the non-monetary incentives scientists have.

The agencies which fund most of the academic biomedical research tend to be focused on certain problem areas and missions related to solving these health issues. Whether it is the institutes at National Institutes of Health (NIH), which each focus on specific areas of health research (e.g., National Institute of Neurological Disorders and Stroke) or non-profit organizations that focus on a particular health problem, these groups have a focus on finding cures and treatments leading to better health outcomes for particular types of patients.

For research administrative offices at universities and elsewhere, the incentives for moving to the use of blockchain applications are speed, efficiency and cost. By reducing costs of university overhead, they will be able to more efficiently facilitate a greater amount of research. This may be important in the coming years at U.S.-based universities especially, where there is a growing interest by federal funding agencies to cap the administrative overhead costs that the universities can charge (in some cases this is currently in excess of 50% on top of federal research grant monies received). The application of blockchain for administrative streamlining would allow the universities using the technology to effectively stay competitive and even expand to a greater amount of research supported with current capabilities.

Non-profit and specific health area focused organizations—such as Fox Foundation for Parkinson's Disease research—that already play a major role in coordinating and facilitating much of the research in their particular area across multiple funding streams and across multiple universities, may become the leading drivers implementing this type of application. The goal here would be for shared efficiency in more rapidly coordinated research to battle the disease in focus for their specific mission.

On the other hand, publishers may at first seem the most disincentivized to move toward new applications of this technology. One of the barriers to adoption in this case is that many envision blockchain potentially disintermediating them from their currently valuable role as the managers of the scientific "blocks" of information in a much more analog way as peer-reviewed publications. But change is inevitable, and many publishers have already been looking to see how to incorporate this technology for short-term efficiency and also to develop capabilities for long-term pivot toward publishing operations more in line with movements by funders and researchers such as the Open Science approach.

Springer Nature and Elsevier, for example, have already begun conducting pilots with the technology, while several other publishers are exploring more fully how this type of DLT can provide more authenticity and transparency to the peer-reviewed process. *Ledger*, a blockchain journal based out of the University of Pittsburgh, became the first journal in 2016 to begin placing all of its content on a blockchain for permanence of the distributed record of authorship.

Other future applications may look at facilitating more rapid peer-review itself, with tracking and authentication via an immutable distributed ledger allowing for a speedier auditability of all pre-publication input, as well as each editing and review step along the way. A shared and open ledger of this process, even with encrypted anonymity where applicable, may open up the peer-review process to more eyes on a single review in faster time. This could be done through some combination of crowdsourcing and weighted scoring. The process would be aligned with traditional credentials (i.e., reviewer status based on professional status and in field publishing) and then expanded to include new junior researcher input with weights of each reviewer constantly graded by peers in the field based on performance. A blockchain layer maintaining this input would allow anyone permissioned to be involved and also to audit the ongoing peer-review activity at any time.

Human research protections (HRP) administrators and their partners on Institutional Review Boards (IRBs) may be traditionally slower and more skeptical toward new technologies.

In the case of blockchain, much of the early administrative value, including transparency, authenticity, encryption and permissioned access, may make them quickly move toward early adoption. Early work by researchers at the University of California San Francisco [14-4] has used a blockchain system with diabetes research data to demonstrate how rapidly and effectively it can be used by multiple parties to audit, verify and authenticate not only the data itself but also details of who has accessed or had access to the data.

This allows more confidence for the regulators on the HIPAA required security of the data, and an almost real-time ability to cheaply and rapidly audit ongoing research in a way that is much more thorough than self-report by the researchers.

An Example of Future Blockchain Application to Peer-Review

The current peer-review system gives only a published/not published signal of confidence. Journal impact scores provide some quasi-confidence in buckets by journal, but these are challenging to track and often hide deeper issues of replicability and reproducibility. Gray literature—such as conference presentations, government studies and industry reports—carry no easy markers of confidence beyond reputation and polished presentations. News reports and press releases on any of the above are often ambiguous, and without further investigation, often superfluous.

But the advent of blockchain/DLT is rapidly leading to new models of incentive and crowdsourcing for expert involved tasks. This tech/human process has matured rapidly in financial and supply chain applications. It is now being matured and tested for applicability to various aspects of health and science.

Distributed, weighted, crowd-tested feedback will provide refined confidence score of multiple types of information in significantly shorter timeframe for a variety of health information. In turn, this will greatly improve the speed and accuracy of information analysis and synthesis, which inform clinical decision-making. If successful, this distributed, blockchain-based peer-review system may be expanded to other areas of science and information. It may become a better, faster template for peer-review.

We can create a crowdsourced peer-review system for health science that would provide faster and more granular confidence scores for a wider variety of health information. This would be done in the context of an incentive system driving both timelines and quality of expert scoring as well as long-term economic sustainability of the model. This system can be created on a blockchain that will enable immutable tracking of changes in related input, management of workflows related to expert confidence score assignment via smart contract and auditable records of scoring to prevent manipulations to the system.

Current confidence in health research is very subjective and consists of (1) all or nothing static confidence score of whether results are published in any peer-reviewed journal, (2) general journal-by-journal confidence based on impact factor of journal, (3) ad hoc, subjective assessment of gray literature, conference presentations, news reports and other miscellaneous delivery of findings.

The use of blockchain will benefit the entire health ecosystem, including the health community of providers; researchers; funding agencies who need to set programmatic priorities; the taxpayers and congressional oversight committees who expect a ROI; the broad community of federal entities, state entities (public health) and local entities that need to make actionable decisions and set policy based on the results coming from the health community.

The impact of the work, if successful, will be the creation and validation of a cost-effective and sustainable new incentive system for expert engagement that can scale across the sciences, where behavioral economics and game theory are applied to mitigate today's opaque and broken incentive models for expert engagement. This model can and will accelerate the assembly of high-quality AI training data that has the potential to ultimately lead to automated assignment of high-value confidence scoring of health research, retrospectively and prospectively.

Chapter 15

The Roadmap

The current system of science is ad hoc, messy, wasteful and still one of the finest systems humans have ever created. Because it is so valuable, we sometimes avoid or forget to look at how we can improve it. But as we have seen, there is tremendous room for improvement using the framework of Open Science along with new tools of blockchain and other emerging tech.

Getting There from Here

What we propose here is a vision of the future of science and what this can look like, along with a rough strategic plan of how to get there. By necessity, this is over-simplified as a way to begin the discussion, planning, execution and implementation of better science. To keep things straightforward, we'll stay primarily focused on the system of federally funded academic health research in the United States, which serves as both global engine and model for much of the remainder of health research. Extrapolation and future expansion of this vision will enable it to be incorporated into other health research systems. We have to start somewhere.

Whenever looking to the future to articulate a vision and map how to get there, it is critical to know where you are now. Once you know where you are and where you want to go, the potential path or paths between the two points become clearer. This can be achieved by using basic project planning principles: identify goal, scope, stakeholders, resources and timeline; assess risks; outline phases; define tasks and subtasks; create milestones and metrics to assess progress; and finally assign tasks and execute. Of course, there are variations to this process, but given the expansive scope and nascent state, we start simply. Here is a preliminary project plan.

This plan is meant as a notional jumping-off point for those stakeholders involved to adjust and build from. Some elements, such as resources, have been left for future discussion, while others represent efforts already underway. Here is a look at some of the early-phase blockchain and health research-related activities already in progress:

Education—Starting with the U.S. Department of Health & Human Services (HHS) Office of the National Coordinator (ONC) white paper contest for blockchain applications in health and research in 2016, there has been a steady stream of education events for blockchain in healthcare with some focus on research throughout the United States and around the world. A few of these have even focused exclusively on research applications such as IEEE clinical trials forums and the Georgetown University/Science Distributed Blockchain for Health Research events. Along with a host of articles in popular literature and on websites on the topic, increasing amounts of peer-reviewed literature has been devoted to the topic of blockchain and research in blockchain-focused journals: *Ledger, Blockchain in Healthcare Today*, *Journal of the British Blockchain Association*, and *Frontiers in Blockchain* (including the special topic area Frontiers: Blockchain for Science). Additional literature on the topic has also been published in traditional journals from *PLoS* to *Nature Communications*. Health Information and Management Systems Society (HIMSS) Blockchain Task Force has established a library that includes research-related items. This book aims to be an expanded and accessible education tool on the topic as well.

Stakeholder engagement (and early pilots)—There are numerous interested parties across federally agencies along with industry, university and non-profit partners discussing, designing, developing and deploying blockchain solutions that are just beginning to achieve some of the promise and value we have outlined. To date, these efforts have been largely bottoming up with only a small amount of coordination. HHS has led the way with its successful Accelerate program for acquisition, and associated engagement of leadership, industry and internal federal stakeholders at HHS and other federal agencies. Other HHS divisions such as the Food & Drug Administration (FDA) and the Center for Disease Control (CDC) have actively been exploring projects for everything from food safety, to pharma supply chain, and different solutions relating to the opioid crisis.

These pockets of interest have begun coalescing into communities of interest across existing working groups relating to areas like precision medicine and supply chain management, along with new health and research focused groups such as those coordinated by the American Council for Technology and Industry Advisory Council (ACT-IAC) and the National Institutes of Health. HIMSS has created a blockchain task force that has had an increasing level of prominence at its large annual conference (30,000+ attendees) and across its worldwide membership (50,000+) of stakeholders across health fields over the past few years.

Research specific engagement is still largely a subset of the health-related interest in blockchain. Early exploration has begun in the pharma industry [15-1] and academia [15-2] with respect to clinical trials. Blockchain and healthcare interest have begun to intersect with organizations more broadly interested in the technology's promise across scientific research such as the non-profits Blockchain for Science and Open Science Organization, as well as the peer-reviewed journal *Frontiers in Blockchain*'s sub-topic, Blockchain for Science. Numerous start-up pilots have begun exploring research-related blockchain applications, especially in the area of publishing [15-3], along with pilots at more established companies such as Springer Nature and Elsevier.

Develop standards (and future framework) —At a Defense Health Agency (DHA) Industry Day briefing by Dr. Manion about the potential of blockchain in health and research in November 2017, the DHA panel agreed on the promise, but noted that widespread piloting and adoption would be unlikely until there was (1) more guidance on the tech from agencies such as the National Institute of Standards and Technology (NIST), (2) more clarity on how blockchain was categorized (e.g., software, infrastructure, etc.) with respect to federal acquisition and cybersecurity standards, (3) more input from federal health regulators and human research protections specialists and (4) progress on standards for the technology by established organizations such as the Institute of Electrical and Electronics Engineers (IEEE).

Work toward these basic criteria is underway for blockchain and its application to health and research. NIST has provided an overview and guidance relating to blockchain [15-4], the FDA has included the tech in its future planning [15-5], and the HHS Office of the Assistant Secretary for Planning and Evaluation has commissioned a report on applications relating to the opioid crisis [15-6] in coordination with the CDC.

When the HHS blockchain-based Accelerate program received its authority to operate in December 2018, it established federal acquisition and cybersecurity standards for the tech. A recent policy review paper published by Frontiers, "Compliance by Design: Regulatory Considerations for Blockchain in Clinical Research" [15-7], gives a comprehensive review on the topic of regulatory considerations along with recommendations for researchers, regulators and policy makers with respect to the tech. It has prompted dialogue on related regulatory issues at several federal agencies.

a. The IEEE Standards Association has also begun leading the way for both tech and data standards for blockchain in healthcare and research with its working group P2418.6—Standard for the Framework of DLT Use in Healthcare and the Life and Social Sciences. This group is developing tech and data standards that align with existing healthcare standards such as Fast Healthcare Interoperability Resources (FHIR) as well as developing blockchain and healthcare standards being developed by other standards agencies such as the International Organization for Standards [15-8]. The IEEE P2418.6 group has also initiated a research sub-working group to explore research-specific data standards that might be required across the more than 200 specialty areas of health and life sciences, such as the common data elements and standards developed for the National Database for Autism Research (NDAR) or the traumatic brain injury research database Federal Interagency Traumatic Brain Injury Research (FITBIR) informatics system. Harmonizing with these established standards in these individual areas and facilitating the development of similar standards for those health research areas that lack them will be crucial for realizing the value that blockchain can bring to research data sharing.

Current State of Health Research

The current state of health research is good, but as we explored earlier, can be improved. This plan is focusing primarily on the $40 billion in U.S. federally funded biomedical/health research executed annually. Briefly, new ideas are generated by 10,000s of principal investigators (PIs) and their 100,000s of post-docs, students and research staff at university, federal, industry and non-profit labs and clinics based on their background knowledge and study of existing literature, knowledge of other ongoing research, and personal observation of lab and clinic phenomena. These ideas are developed with collaborators into proposals for intramural (government to government lab) or extramural (government to non-government lab) funding and submitted into the systems specific to the funding agency. This proposal submission is sometimes in response to a specific call for proposals and other times is for more general windows of proposal submission. Proposals are generally vetted and signed off by several administrative and regulatory offices at the PIs' affiliated institutions prior to submission (Figure 15.1).

In addition to the roughly $40 billion available in federal research funds each year, there is an even greater level of internal industry funding (mostly pharma) for advanced research and development that is based similarly on the existing literature but is frequently not widely reported as it is proprietary and focused on developing drugs or devices for sale. For the purposes of this environmental scan we will not be looking directly at this bucket of research. How and where proprietary industry research fits into this picture is a different and more complex picture that will be tackled in later work. Proposals that seek to simply push this market-driven proprietary research into the transparent public sphere with academic research overlook the simple fact that elimination of the existing profit motive for industry would also eliminate the motivation to invest in this costly and high-risk research. It is an important part of the ecosystem that we should keep in mind but is a different phylum entirely.

There are also smaller amounts of academic and non-profit funds available for research. These can be treated as augmentations to the federally funded research dollars as though some specifics of the funding awards may differ, and the results generally contribute to the same overall output and body of literature. It should be noted that many non-profits that fund research have a specific health issue as their mission. This concentrated area of focus for these non-profit organizations and their associated patient,

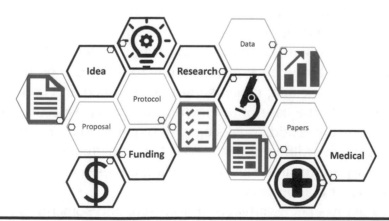

Figure 15.1   Current system: key stakeholders and connections of the current system with a highlight on critical stakeholders.

advocate, provider and researcher community of interests can sometimes make them faster to move as a network into new areas of innovation. These organizations will be pivotal later when we describe the path to future goals. Their early adoption can accelerate the enterprise-wide evaluation and implementation of blockchain-based solutions.

Moving back to the system of science, proposals are screened by administrative staff for completeness and programmatic fit and then assigned to volunteer subject matter experts (SMEs) for review. The SMEs score the proposals and then convene to discuss and rank the proposals for funding, generally based on predetermined guidelines relating to quality, feasibility and impact. PIs and their affiliated organizations are notified of their award and then funds are distributed. This distribution often occurs with a significant percentage of overhead costs (10%–50+%) also going to the affiliated organization to cover administrative and infrastructure costs.

Funded research proposals are developed into formal research protocols, outlining all specific details of the research to be undertaken. Before research can begin, PIs must receive formal approval from the university's appropriate research regulatory body, the Institutional Review Board (IRB) for human research or the Institutional Animal Care and Use Committee for basic animal research. Even research looking at existing healthcare and/or human research data requires regulatory signoff to confirm appropriate privacy protections for patients, though this is often expedited. This approval can in different circumstances be sought and even received before the proposal is funded, though any changes made to the associated protocol must be approved by the regulatory body as an amendment or updated and approved as a new protocol.

As research execution gets underway, there are wide variations in details and time frame depending on the research specifics. Basically, experiments or clinical observations are conducted, and data is collected based on a predetermined data governance plan outlined in the protocol. In cases of prospective clinical research, patients must be recruited and consented for their involvement. In the case of research involving retrospective looks at existing data sometimes additional steps are required to access the data, especially if it sits in a different institution. This usually requires demonstration of regulatory approval, details of the planned research and demonstration of feasibility or competency.

Once the data has been gathered or accessed, and sometimes at interim steps (e.g., 50%) along the way in some longer studies, analysis begins based on plan described in the protocol. Initial data management sometimes requires data processing including combining data, data cleaning, standard-ization, normalization or other general steps. There are quality control and assurance checks along the way as outlined in the protocol.

Data analysis can vary but should follow the prescribed statistical tests outlined in the protocol, testing against the initial hypotheses. This adher-ence to include additional test with appropriate justification and notation is critical to provide valuable and reproducible research. Simply running an array of tests on a data set until something interesting or statistically signifi-cant shows up (commonly referred to as p-hacking) is far too frequently done without understanding (or not caring) that resulting "significant" results are more likely false positives. This is quietly one of the most promi-nent weak points in research, resulting in the perpetuation of questionable results.

Results of the statistical analyses, often retested for validation, are then looked at in the context of the study and other research to interpret what it means. These findings are based not only on the analysis of the study data, but also on known limitations to the study as well as support or con-tradiction of other findings in the literature. Much like the initial ideas and hypotheses, this step in the research has some of the most subjectivity and creativity from the PI and senior researchers. It is also an area of potential over (or sometimes under) estimation of what the results mean in real-world terms. It is here that interaction with colleagues and other experts in the particular sub-field is critical to help confirm, refine or reject the initial determination of findings.

This peer interaction happens in several steps, first locally or with known colleagues involved in similar research. Through personal communica-tions, lab meetings and local presentation of findings, feedback is received to refine how the research results are interpreted. If a major oversight is noticed it can mean revisiting or even reproducing the research. Generally solid research done with full knowledge of the supporting body of literature will move forward to next being presented at the national or international level with the broader community of interest at a professional conference or some other venue. This allows more refinement and feedback, as well as beginning to inform colleagues about the new findings.

At this point, research findings are ready for submission to a peer-reviewed journal. This is an intensive process of formal preparation with the context and reference to the supporting body of literature. The goal of this formal process of publication is to introduce the findings to the broader community as a fixed and appropriately supported addition to the overall

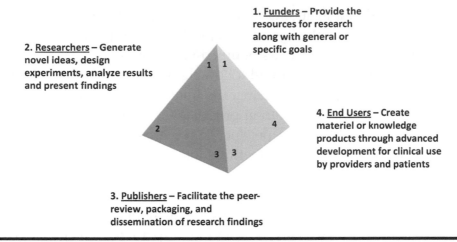

Figure 15.2   Four-sided platform of science.

body of knowledge from which all future research will be launched. This body of peer-reviewed literature is the immutable ledger, or blockchain of science. As noted in the brief thought experiment post, "Proof of Science" [15-9] (Figure 15.2):

> The Blockchain of Science has been running for 300 years. It is not exactly tech, though significant portions have been digitized. It is the ad-hoc collection of scientific papers published in the peer-reviewed body of literature. These are hashed (i.e. referenced) and represented in subsequent blocks (i.e. papers) to form a chain (i.e. body of knowledge). The consensus mechanism? Peer-review. Proof of Science.
>
> This isn't a mere thought experiment or loose analogy. This is a conceptual framework for those that [sic] understand blockchain/ DLT to understand what science is at its core, and for scientists to understand what the newly maturing field of blockchain/DLT can do for science.

Future Vision of Health Research

The possibilities and potential pitfalls of the future are endless. It isn't necessarily new ideas that will transform science, as much as it will be existing ideas combined with the capabilities that new technological tools can bring. In the near term, 5–10 years, an Open Science framework combined with the capabilities of blockchain working in synergy with other emerging tech tools such as machine learning can provide a host of rapid improvement of the speed, cost and quality of health research. This will accelerate the advancement of medicine and improve our ability to save lives and improve health outcomes and quality of life.

The biggest barriers will also be old ideas: bureaucracy, resistance to change and lack of political will from leadership in all types of organizations involved in research and knowledge translation. To overcome these, we'll need to see external validation of the value of blockchain applied to other industries and areas of healthcare. We have already begun to see this over the last few years. In 2016, prior to the HHS ONC white paper contest exploring the possibilities for blockchain in health and research, not many in these areas had heard the word, much less had a sense of the myriad ways it could transform the industry. Now, just a few years later the state of blockchain in healthcare has gone from conceptual to real-world applications at HHS and across the industry, already transforming everything from purchasing (HHS Accelerate) and insurance remittance (Change Healthcare) to tracking medical devices/adverse events (Spiritus Partners) and providing cancer drugs that would otherwise be thrown away to those most in need (Good Shepherd Pharmacy and RemediChain). Given the potential for research, it seems inevitable that transformation will sweep through health research and its current challenges. The only question is how quickly.

Here are some of the main areas in health research where the application of blockchain technology will have the most impact in the next 5–10 years:

1. **Sharing ideas/hypotheses**—Currently, the ability of the average researcher or administrator to look across all ideas/hypotheses in the system of federal research begins at funding when information is available in sites like National Institutes of Health (NIH) Reporter and Clinicaltrials.gov. This system can be enhanced beyond the current state of self-report by automated extraction and processing via smart contract application. Further, with immutable timestamping to validate researcher contribution and real-time peer-to-peer sharing between researchers and admins akin to that between buyers in the HHS Accelerate program, ideas/hypotheses submitted for federal funding can be shared upon submission. This will allow for a host of new possibilities of coordination, collaboration and avoiding undesired replication among researcher that in the current system may not even have been funded. Imagine not wasting hundreds of hours preparing a proposal for an

idea that was already rejected or joining forces with another researcher with a similar idea for a successful bid/project.

2. **Accelerated proposal review**—Similar to the 2016 federal GSA pilot which demonstrated reduction in vendor proposal review time by 90%, a blockchain layer across the legacy systems involved in grant proposal review at federal agencies could significantly speed up submission to award time while reducing administrative costs. Tracking and validation of data elements involved in submitting a proposal could also allow for pre-population of new submissions, saving time and effort on the part of researchers reapplying from federal agencies. Cost savings could even be carried back to the universities as they integrate into the system, reducing administrative burden.

3. **Funding innovations**—There are a variety of innovations related to funding that could also be worked into the future state. These include more reliable and automated expenditure tracking for research grant dollars. This would provide reduction in waste and fraud in the short term, with a more accurate longitudinal picture of what grant dollars contribute directly and indirectly to medical advances and improved outcomes over years and multiple budget cycles. There would also be innovations in shared agency funding or even crowdfunding by non-profits, private companies and individuals to support specific research.

4. **Protocol development**—Rapid, automated protocol development from data elements pulled from proposals and/or validated elements from previous research that are then processed and pre-populated via smart contract could reduce time and effort by researchers.

5. **Regulatory value**—Enhanced, automated facilitation of submissions for regulatory approval, in addition to more comprehensive document tracking via a shared ledger would significantly speed up the time for approval, while reducing the time and effort for researchers and regulators. Rapid, automated auditing of studies with less dependence on researcher self-report would greatly improve human research protection staff to ensure compliance without new burden on the researchers.

6. **Enhanced data sharing**—The ability to share permissioned (automatic check for valid IRB-approved) access to cloud-based data will allow for tremendous expansion of qualified research eyes on a health problem area. A distributed immutable ledger will allow a record of who created each data point, how it was collected, how it was analyzed, who has touched it since and what hypotheses it has been tested against. This would be rapidly and cheaply auditable by researchers, admins

and regulators to quickly check and verify the validity of findings. This would also incorporate a system of timestamping and contribution tracking for those who have done work on every stage from ideation to peer-review of findings for appropriate credit. This would look something like a Wikipedia page for each data set, with authenticity and provenance of every data point. This data tracking would allow for cleaner and more appropriate data aggregation across studies and associated meta-analyses.

7. **Methods and analyses tracking**—Much like the HHS Accelerate program has allowed peer-to-peer sharing of purchasing details, providing strategic buying information to federal buyers at their fingertips, there could be a similar database for researchers in every area. This would allow rapid searching of automatically extracted data from every federally reviewed and/or funded study to see (1) what methods have been used with which variations, (2) by which researchers and where current capabilities are and (3) with what success and contribution to shared databases. This would allow researchers to pre-select alignment to existing methodology where incremental contribution to the established research in the field is the goal, or deliberate divergence when new directions are warranted.

8. **Pre-review of interpretations**—Similar to currently available pre-publication sites like ArXiv.org and Biorxiv.org, which allow individuals to get feedback on their work pre-publication, a crowdsourced open network could expand this to interpretation of results feedback earlier in the process. A distributed layer of verification of identity of users would allow better weighting where appropriate (feedback from a seasoned researcher in the field may carry more weight than an inexperienced graduate student, though group feedback on comments from each could also shift this weight), while also giving an authenticated record of reviewer feedback that could be transferred to the formal peer-review process once the publication is ready; like transferring college credits. This system could incorporate existing identity solutions for users like Open Researcher and Contributor ID (ORCID) digital identifier (iD) or the federal contractor System for Award Management (SAM), or develop a new system as needed for identity verification and management.

9. **Crowdsourced peer-review**—Building from the existing pre-publication approach and the earlier precursor of result interpretation feedback mentioned in #8, the process of open, crowdsourced, weighted peer-review

could be widely integrated into the system. This three-stage system would have the effect of opening research to a wider audience at stages like (1) small lab meeting group feedback on interpretation of results, (2) conference-type feedback on more comprehensive pre-publication findings and (3) a crowdsourced weighted peer-review. The blockchain layer would simply provide authenticity of input at each layer with more rapid processing (e.g., weighted scoring) and auditable continuity.

10. **Fractionalized publishing**—Further advancing the speed with which health research is conducted would be a system of fractionalized publishing, or moving data, results and findings to review and publication sooner and in smaller increments. Currently, publications lean toward larger studies and combined findings to meet a level of attention required to stand out from the crowd of competitors for higher ranked (and more often read) journals. This tendency in turn delays publications, can bias interpretations and frequently leaves out critical negative findings. The lack of negative findings reported in the literature is especially detrimental to progress and research funding ROI, given that many studies that don't produce actionable findings are repeated unnecessarily with no knowledge of or comparison to previous efforts that went unpublished. By breaking publication of findings into more bite-size increments and shifting the broader narrative to later stages of knowledge translation, we would shift to a system of building a foundation of scientific knowledge from pieces ranging from pebbles to boulders, to a more standardized size of bricks.

The Open Science framework has already considered and conceptualized all of these ideas. Many pilot attempts are underway. In most instances, the goal of the pilot is technologically feasible without a distributed solution. What blockchain provides is a layer of trust and auditability to each system, along with the speeding of automation of processes (and removal of slow and biased intermediaries) via smart contracts. It also allows for interoperability of these systems for a combined efficiency far beyond what the individual parts could achieve.

Blockchain changes the value proposition for adoption of these advances at the individual and combined level in a way that incentivizes key stakeholder to support them at an earlier stage. Current technology hasn't achieved this because much of the challenge is with motivating people, organizations and networks to buy-in and contribute to the shared governance required at each step.

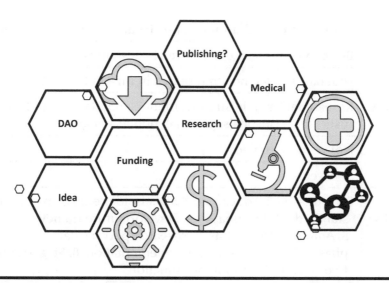

Figure 15.3   Future vision: DAO of science.

Together, these advances can create an efficient, cost-reducing, lifesaving learning health research system that supplies higher quality evidence for advances in medical treatment and health outcomes. This would be a preliminary stage of moving toward a distributed autonomous organization (DAO) for health research, continuing to utilize trusted, centralized intermediaries where necessary, until the governance system itself is refined and trusted enough to replace them with open, fully crowdsourced controlled systems. While this may require more advanced platforms, governance structures and distributed protocol than are currently available to be fully implemented in the near term, these initial steps are achievable in the next 5–10 years. They will likely come about inevitably, but this will happen sooner and in a more integrated fashion with the right stakeholder engagement (Figure 15.3).

Roadmap

As we saw in Table 15.1, there are a number of milestones that outline some of the basic steps toward this future goal. How quickly and widespread this is achieved will depend on key stakeholder engagement and coordination. This strategic plan toward better science, cheaper research and faster miracles is just an outline to get the discussion moving forward with a shared vision. The specifics of that vision and the granular steps to get there will

Table 15.1   Preliminary Project Plan for Better Health Research via Blockchain

Goal	Better health science, improved health outcomes
Scope	Federally funded health research in the United States
Stakeholders	Researchers, administrators, funders, regulators, publishers, end users (e.g., Hospitals, pharma), public, congress
Resources	Not yet determined
Timeline	5–10 years
Phases and major tasks	Early phase—1. Education, 2. Stakeholder engagement, 3. Develop standards; Active phase—4. Develop future framework, 5. Administrative pilots, 6. Research pilots; Final phase—7. Refinement and implementation, 8. Staged shift to distributed autonomous function
Milestones	Cross-agency working groups, % university engagement, IEEE/NIST standards, future framework, successful admin pilot, successful research pilots, enterprise deployment, stages to DAO
Metrics	Number of agencies/programs in working group, number of universities engaged, number of fields with data standards, % buy-in future framework, number of pilots and % success, data quality, speed of access, reproducibility, real-time tracking speed, translation time, health money saved, improvement in health outcomes.

be determined by individuals and groups involved, not by this book or any other singular vision.

The most critical stakeholders are the researchers themselves, though funding agencies, publishers, university administrators, providers, hospitals and healthcare systems are also necessary, particularly to determine how rapidly advances can occur. And of course, the patients and their advocates are the key group of end users for driving the momentum forward. Of all the federal agencies, NIH will be the most crucial given that it manages the bulk of federal health funding, but other agencies, including the DoD and U.S. Department of Veterans Affairs can also play a pivotal role in early adoption for health issues such as traumatic brain injury where there is already advanced infrastructure for coordination, the agencies have mission-related needs for more rapid medical advances and the research areas are more tightly connected to the health delivery systems.

This roadmap is only a starting point, and these are a few markers and milestones for the later phases along the way:

1. **Cross-agency, public–private, subject matter working groups—** Dialogue across federal agencies is critical, and eventually these will need to occur along specific health subject matter/health issue lines to dive deeper into early use areas and facilitate adoption by associated research and advocacy groups. Traumatic brain injury and autism seem like potential early adopters based on their existing federal research registry framework and standardization. Other early candidates may come from health issues with strong advocacy groups and research networks like Cystic Fibrosis, Cerebral Palsy and Parkinson's Disease.

2. **University and research group engagement—**There are nearly 300 universities along with hospitals, non-profit organizations and a few other private organizations that receive $10 million or more in federal health research funding each year. Engagement and early discussion with researchers, administrators, regulators and information technology staff at these locations will facilitate more rapid development and implementation of any plan. Getting 50–75 of these NIH-funded organizations as early adopters involved in planning representing the larger, smaller and unique types of organizations would provide a solid foundation for the active phase.

3. **IEEE/NIST standards—**Continued work on and development of standards will be critical. This will be most effective if the federal agencies involved along with the early adopting research organizations are also involved. Technical standards should be harmonized with other existing technology standards, and data and taxonomic standards should be individualized as needed to specific health areas with unique data elements. These should also be aligned with existing data standards for each area (e.g., Clinical Data Interchange Standards Consortium (CDISC) and Federal Interagency Traumatic Brain Injury Research (FITBIR) informatics system standards for traumatic brain injury). Considerations for need of additional standards for each phase of science beyond data gathering, such as methodological and publishing, should also be considered. This will be important toward development of future governance standards.

4. **Future framework—**With early-phase steps underway and learning from the above (#1–3), a more comprehensive strategic planning effort should be undertaken to develop a detailed future framework for an integrated, distributed system of health research. This should include representation from many of the above-mentioned groups, while balancing for broad input versus speed of development and consensus.

It may be useful to draw from previously successful strategic planning efforts while avoiding the traditional pitfalls of "we've always done it this way." An iterative, continuous integration approach to this will allow for early speed, with more broad input toward consensus achieved at later stages. This will become a learning template for later governance discussions.

5. **Successful admin pilots**—Just like the successful HHS Accelerate program, which was executed at the cost of $2–3 million and a ROI of 800%–1,000% and which went from concept to sandbox to live deployment in under a year, administrative pilots will be more easily achieved to build capabilities and develop trust in the technology. These can be encouraged through smaller bundles of funding but will also require buy-in of leadership and key stakeholders for each. Human-centered design incorporating existing processes and input from stakeholders has been a successful model that should be encouraged.

6. **Regulatory engagement**—Engagement and policy planning with health regulators must precede any widespread testing or adoption of clinical research applications involving population health information (PHI). An outline of what this looks like has been published in more detail in "Blockchain Compliance by Design: Regulatory Considerations for Blockchain for Clinical Research," Charles et al.

7. **Successful research pilots**—Funding for rapid research pilots should be encouraged across health areas and individual institutions at NIH. Those involving multiple institutions and existing research networks will be most valuable. A variety of pilots should be rolled out with a coordinated system of sharing and lessons learned.

8. **Enterprise deployment**—Those models and networks that demonstrate success can become early templates for rolling out more comprehensive and integrated systems (i.e., administrative and data elements incorporating multiple blockchain applications in a single network). How and where this next level of deployment occurs should be more finely articulated in the future framework planning (#4) with the early pilots serving as subjects for something like an adaptive trial; certain milestones being met trigger advanced application and expansion.

9. **Stages to DAO**—As noted previously, there will be stages of development toward creation of a DAO, with many centralized portions remaining as scaffolding until there is consensus based on predetermined milestones that these can be disintermediated. Future planning in #4 can give a more detailed picture of what this looks like.

Future

Nothing that will transform the world will do so without itself being transformed. The current models of research and concepts of blockchain and distributed systems can—and should—be taken apart and reconstructed in whatever forms are most viable for mission success: saving lives and better health. The scientific, medical, government funding and technology communities all have their own versions of "it has always been done this way" or getting caught up in semantics rather than solutions. This needs to be anticipated as a known bias and worked past, in order to create new models and transformative change. Of course, there are additional biases that will need to be taken into consideration, such as socio-economic ones.

Dr. Tiffany Gray, DrPh, MPH, public health & research advisor, tells us that for example when it comes to access to information, like telehealth, users tend to be educated, have already access. "We need to make sure we go to the users who don't and engage them more; teach them how to navigate the system better. We want to make sure that the technologies and what we do with them don't further disparities within populations. People have raised concerns with AI about racism, discrimination, so we have to make sure that we don't create new disparities. Public health needs to be key component."

The goals and steps outlined in this book are a starting point, not an endpoint. Further into the future, in a decade or two, these steps may lead to additional opportunities to advance the system of health research. The data standardization achieved through the shared governance of blockchain solutions will enable more rapid advances in artificial intelligence and machine learning applied to health research and medicine. This can facilitate more reliable and rapid knowledge translation, which is currently bottlenecked by the sheer volume of information and uneven distribution in confidence of even the top peer-reviewed tier. This will enable feedback into the education system, augmenting learning and decision-making of everything from early pre-med and science education to continuing education of providers and personalized education of patients and their advocates.

Further dissection and reimagining of the process of knowledge creation, translation, policy development and personalized health decision-making will be transformed in ways almost unimaginable in just a few decades. Students may contribute to scientific research by playing video games. The public may provide constant streams of personal health data (when and where they consent, and possibly for economic gain directly or through tokenization) for a continual learning health system that is largely automated. Scientific publications may become an artifact of history as crowdsourced research is automatically converted into provider decision-making augmentation facilitated by artificial intelligence.

We have moved beyond the pure speculation of science fiction on these matters and have entered a time when the best ideas that may not have been achievable are now in reach with the appropriate application of new technological tools. With the outline in this book we hope we have provided the basis of a system-wide leap forward in health and medicine that will improve health and save lives. Better science. Faster miracles.

Notes

Introduction

1. Manion, S.T. (2017, 16 January). Science Will Be Blockchained by 2025. *LinkedIn Pulse*. Retrieved from: www.linkedin.com/pulse/science-blockchained-2025-sean-manion.

Chapter 1

1. Nakamoto, S. (2008, 01 November). Bitcoin: A Peer-To-Peer Electronic Cash System. *Bitcoin.org*. Retrieved from: https://bitcoin.org/bitcoin.pdf.
2. May, T.C. (1994, 10 September). The Cyphernomicon: Cypherpunks FAQ and More, Version 0.666. Cypherpunks.to. Retrieved from: https://nakamotoinstitute.org/static/docs/cyphernomicon.txt.
3. Bell, J.D. (1996). "Assassination Politics". In Schwartau, W. (ed.). *Information Warfare* (2nd ed.). New York: Thunder's Mouth Press. pp. 420–425.
4. Stephenson, N. (1999). *Cryptonomicon*. New York: Avon Press.
5. Oberhaus, D. (2018, 27 August). The World's Oldest Blockchain Has Been Hiding in the New York Times Since 1995. *Motherboard*. Retrieved from: www.vice.com/en_us/article/j5nzx4/what-was-the-first-blockchain.
6. Haber, S., Stornetta, W.S. (1991). How to time-stamp a digital document. *Journal of Cryptology* 3, 99–111.

Chapter 2

1. Bailey, J. (2018, 30 July). Art World, Meet Blockchain. *Artnome*. Retrieved from: www.artnome.com/news/2018/7/21/art-world-meet-blockchain
2. Bizouati-Kennedy, Y. (2018, 12 November). What Would Van Gogh Say About Blockchain? *BlockTV*. Retrieved from: www.blocktv.com/article/2018-11-12/5be9f65bf403c-women-pose-with-willem-de-kooning-art.

3. SaveonSend. (2019, 03 November). Does Bitcoin/Blockchain Make Sense for International Money Transfers? *SaveonSend*. Retrieved from: www.saveonsend. com/blog/bitcoin-blockchain-money-transfer/.

Chapter 3

1. Kamath, R. (2018, 12 June). Food traceability on blockchain: Walmart's pork and mango pilots with IBM. Journal of the British Blockchain Association vol 1, Issue 1, page 3712. Retrieved from: https://jbba.scholasticahq.com/article/3712-food-traceability-on-blockchain-walmart-s-pork-and-mango-pilots-with-ibm.
2. Blockchain in Transport Alliance (BITA). www.bita.studio/
3. Manion, S.T. (2019). "Advancing Health Research with Blockchain". In Dhillon, V., Bass, J., Hooper, M., Metcalf, D., Cahana, A. (eds.). *Blockchain in Healthcare: Innovations that Empower Patients, Connect Professionals and Improve Care* (1st ed.). Productivity Press/CRC Press.
4. HHS ONC Blockchain Challenge White Paper Contest Winners. www. cccinnovationcenter.com/challenges/block-chain-challenge/view-winners/.
5. Rockwell, M. (2019, 16 August). HHS Accelerate to Launch in January. *Gcn. com*. Retrieved from: https://gcn.com/articles/2019/08/16/hhs-accelerate.aspx.
6. Remedichain. www.remedichain.com/#/home.

Chapter 4

1. Manion, S.T. (2018, 19 April). 3-Dimensional Blockchain: Oeuf-Dimensional Blockchain Theory. *Linkedin Pulse*. Retrieved from: www.linkedin.com/pulse/3-dimensional-blockchain-oeuf-dimensional-theory-sean-manion.

Chapter 5

1. Bass, J. (2019, 28 January). The Truth about Blockchain and Its Application to Health Care. *Hfma.org*. www.hfma.org/topics/hfm/2019/february/63125.html.

Chapter 6

1. ResearchAmerica. (2016). Factsheet - Investment in Research Saves Money and Lives. *ResearchAmerica*.org. Retrieved from: www.researchamerica.org/polls-and-publications/fact-sheets#investment.
2. UNESCO Institute for Statistics. (2019). How Much Does Your Country Invest in R&D? *uis.unesco.org*. Retrieved form: http://uis.unesco.org/apps/visualisations/research-and-development-spending/.

Chapter 7

1. Manion, S.T. (2018, 21 February). Enhancing Federal Research: Traumatic Brain Injury & Blockchain Technology - Part 1.5, The Why. *LinkedIn Pulse*. Retrieved from: www.linkedin.com/pulse/ enhancing-federal-research-traumatic-brain-injury-part-sean-manion-1.
2. Sparks, J. (2002). Timeline of Laws Related to the Protection of Human Subjects. *History.nih.gov*. Retrieved from: https://history.nih.gov/about/ timelines_laws_human.html.
3. Morris, Z.S. et al. (2011 December). The answer is 17 years, what is the question: Understanding time lags in translational research. *Journal of the Royal Society of Medicine* vol 104, Issue 12, pages 510–520. Retrieved from: www.ncbi.nlm.nih.gov/pmc/articles/PMC3241518/.
4. Vargesson, N. (2015, 04 June). Thalidomide-induced teratogenesis: History and mechanisms. *Birth Defects Research Part C: Embryo Today: Reviews* vol 105, Issue 2, pages 140–156. Retrieved from: www.ncbi.nlm.nih.gov/pmc/articles/ PMC4737249/.

Chapter 8

1. Freedman, L.P. et al. (2015, 19 June). Economics of reproducibility in preclinical research. *PLoS Biology* vol 13, Issue 6, page e1002165. Retrieved from: https://journals.plos.org/plosbiology/article?id=10.1371/journal. pbio.1002165.
2. Yong, E. (2018, 19 November). Psychology's Replication Crisis Is Running Out of Excuses. *The Atlantic*. Retrieved from: www.theatlantic.com/science/ archive/2018/11/psychologys-replication-crisis-real/576223/.
3. Reardon, S. (2018, 29 October). US Government Halts Heart Stem-Cell Study. *Nature News*. Retrieved from: www.nature.com/articles/d41586-018-07232-0.
4. Eggerston, L. (2010, 09 March). Lancet retracts 12-year-old article linking autism to MMR vaccines. *Canadian Medical Association Journal* vol. 182, Issue 4, pages E199–E200. Retrieved from: www.ncbi.nlm.nih.gov/pmc/articles/ PMC2831678/.

Chapter 9

1. Buranyi, S. (2017, 27 June). Is the Staggeringly Profitable Business of Scientific Publishing Bad for Science? *The Guardian*. Retrieved from: www.theguardian.com/science/2017/jun/27/ profitable-business-scientific-publishing-bad-for-science.

2. Else, H. (2019, 30 May). Ambitious Open-Access Plan S Delayed to Let Research Community Adapt. *Nature News.* Retrieved from: www.nature.com/articles/d41586-019-01717-2.

Chapter 11

1. Freedman, L.P. et al. (2015, 19 June). Economics of reproducibility in pre-clinical research. *PLoS Biology* vol 13, Issue 6, page e1002165. Retrieved from: https://journals.plos.org/plosbiology/article?id=10.1371/journal.pbio.1002165.
2. Brainard, J. and You, J. (2018, 25 October). What a massive database of retracted papers reveals about science publishing's 'death penalty'. *Science* vol 25, Issue 1, pages 1–5. Retrieved from: www.sciencemag.org/news/2018/10/what-massive-database-retracted-papers-reveals-about-science-publishing-s-death-penalty.
3. Chawla, D.S. (2018, 05 June). Can Auditing Scientific Research Help Fix Its Reproducibility Crisis? *Pacific Standard.* https://psmag.com/news/can-auditing-scientific-research-help-fix-its-reproducibility-crisis.
4. Payakachat, N. et al. (2016, February). National database for autism research (NDAR): Big data opportunities for health services research and health technology assessment. *Pharmacoeconomics* vol 34, Issue 2, pages 127–138. Retrieved from: www.ncbi.nlm.nih.gov/pmc/articles/PMC4761298/.

Chapter 12

1. Macilwain, C. (2010, 09 June). Science economics: What science is really worth? *Nature* vol 465, pages 682–684. Retrieved from: www.nature.com/articles/465682a.
2. Guthrie S. et al. (2014). Estimating the Economic Returns on Cancer Research in the UK. *RAND Europe.* Retrieved from: www.rand.org/randeurope/research/projects/economic-returns-on-cancer-research.html.
3. Guthrie, S. et al. (2018). Evidence Synthesis on Measuring the Distribution of Benefits of Research and Innovation. *The Royal Society.* Retrieved from: www.rand.org/pubs/research_reports/RR2610z1.html.
4. Johnson, J.L. and Manion, S.T. (2019, December. Blockchain in Healthcare, Research, and Scientific Publishing. *Medical Writing, EMWA.* Volume 28, Issue 4.

Chapter 13

1. Thornton, D. (2017, 16 November). GSA Experimenting with Blockchain to Cut Contracting Time. *Federal News Network*. Retrieved from: https://federalnewsnetwork.com/it-modernization-2017/2017/11/gsa-experimenting-with-blockchain-to-cut-contracting-time/.
2. Fernandez, R. (2010, 24 September). Barriers to Open Science: From Big Business to Watson and Crick. *Opensource.com*. Retrieved from: https://opensource.com/business/10/8/barriers-open-science-big-business-watson-and-crick.

Chapter 14

1. U.S. Securities and Exchange Commission. (2017, 25 July). SEC Issues Investigative Report Concluding DAO Tokens, a Digital Asset, Were Securities. *Sec.gov*. www.sec.gov/news/press-release/2017-131.
2. Blockchain for Science: www.blockchainforscience.com/
3. National Science Board. (2016). Science and Engineering Indicators 2016. *National Science Board*. Retrieved from: www.nsf.gov/statistics/2016/nsb20161/#/report/front-matter.
4. Wong, D.R. et al. (2019, 22 February). Prototype of running clinical trials in an untrustworthy environment using blockchain. *Nature Communications* vol 10, page 917. Retrieved from: www.nature.com/articles/s41467-019-08874-y.

Chapter 15

1. Lynch, M. (2019, 14 February). Boehringer Ingelheim and IBM Bring Blockchain to Clinical Trials. *Outsourcing-pharma.com*. Retrieved from: www.outsourcing-pharma.com/Article/2019/02/14/Boehringer-Ingelheim-and-IBM-bring-blockchain-to-clinical-trials.
2. Wong, D.R. et al. (2019, 22 February). Prototype of running clinical trials in an untrustworthy environment using blockchain. *Nature Communications* vol 10, page 917. Retrieved from: www.nature.com/articles/s41467-019-08874-y.
3. Mackey, T.K. et al. (2019, 30 October). A Framework Proposal for Blockchain-Based Scientific Publishing Using Shared Governance. *Frontiers in Blockchain, Blockchain for Distributed Research*. Retrieved from: www.frontiersin.org/articles/10.3389/fbloc.2019.00019/full.
4. Yaga, D. et al. (2018). Blockchain Technology Overview. *National Institute of Standards and Technology Publications*. Retrieved from: https://nvlpubs.nist.gov/nistpubs/ir/2018/NIST.IR.8202.pdf.

5. Aniyikaiye, E. (2019, 13 September). The FDA Looks Inward as It Tackles Interoperability. *National Law Review*. Retrieved from: www.natlawreview. com/article/fda-looks-inward-it-tackles-interoperability.
6. Dullabh, P. et al. (2019 (expected)). Potential Uses of Blockchain Technology for Outcomes Research on Opioids. *HHS Office of the Assistant Secretary for Planning and Evaluation*. In progress.
7. Charles, W. et al. (2019, 08 November). Blockchain Compliance by Design: Regulatory Considerations for Blockchain in Clinical Research. *Frontiers in Blockchain, Blockchain for Science*. Retrieved from: www.frontiersin.org/ articles/10.3389/fbloc.2019.00018/full.
8. P2418.6-Standard for the Framework of Distributed Ledger Technology (DLT) Use in Healthcare and the Life and Social Sciences. Retrieved from: https:// standards.ieee.org/project/2418_6.html.
9. Manion, S.T. (2019, 16 January). Proof of Science. *Science Distributed – Talk*. Retrieved from: https://sciencedistributed.com/talk/f/proof-of-science.

Index